I Thought You Had Retired

Joel D. Glover

I Thought You Had Retired

ISBN: 978-0-9600469-8-0 (Paperback)
ISBN: 978-0-9600469-9-7 (ePub)
Also available for Kindle

Book design and layout: Lighthouse24

Dedication

Well folks, it's been a wild ride. With me being in the wildlife section, many in the enforcement section did not appreciate my law enforcement efforts. While enforcement wasn't originally my priority, I embraced it and worked hard to apprehend violators. My success was due to training from veteran officers who accepted me as an officer and my willingness to put forth the effort needed to make the apprehensions.

When the two veteran game wardens in our county retired, I took on a new role of training officer. It was a somewhat peculiar situation. I quickly learned to embrace the role of teacher. I found myself understanding how my wife could enjoy being a classroom teacher for so many years. There is a lot of gratification in seeing a student grasp an idea or concept. There is a tremendous satisfaction when you see them put something you have taught them into practice. I have been fortunate to witness this many times. I have officers, who became my supervisors, tell me that a wise man once told them...in reference to something I taught them. There is a lot of gratification in that.

In this book you will read about some of my efforts to train new officers. After I retired and then came back part-time, I found myself doing investigations and training new officers. I loved it.

While I often referred to them as kids, that was not a jab at them, it was that when compared to me, most of them were kids.

I'm sure the officers who trained me thought of me as a kid. Of course, I was a kid and they were ancient. Good grief some were forty years old!

My career has been a wild ride. Luckily, I wasn't in it alone. Through the hard times and through all the various coworkers there was one strong pillar that I leaned on. My wonderful wife was there supporting me 100 percent. I could not have asked for a better partner in life. I am so richly blessed to have her by my side and I praise God for her each day. I dedicate this book to her. I love you babe.

Disclaimer

The stories in this book are true to the best of my knowledge and recollection. I changed many of the names. I'm certain you will find some of these stories difficult to believe. As I've said before, I found them hard to believe and I was there! These are my stories for your enjoyment. If you think you recognize someone in here, it's probably just your imagination.

Contents

Where's Your Passenger?

THERE IS NO SUBSTITUTE for being in the right place at the right time. As a game warden trying to cover 652 square miles, the chances of being in that right place are normally slim and none. During the deer season it is often difficult to decide where to work. I guess I should explain the difficult part is deciding which of the many complaint areas to work in. While Coosa County is not as large as many counties, it still takes nearly an hour to get from one corner to the other. That being true, when you received a complaint and you were close by, you tended to get a little excited.

On a cold late January night, Conservation Enforcement Officer (CEO) Drake Hayes and I had been working night hunting on the east side of Coosa County. It was late in the season and working day and night was taking its toll on both of us. Of course, the fact that he was half my age made it a little easier on him! I had been working five years when he was born. When you put it like that it sort of makes me sound old.

Not having any activity by midnight, I called Drake and told him I was thinking I would head toward the house. He said he was thinking the same thing. Just because we were headed in did not mean we would go straight home. We each would take a route through areas where deer were known to frequent in hopes of running up on a spotlighter or someone else up to no good.

Although it didn't happen often, every once in a while, even a blind hog would find an acorn.

At 12:41 a.m. the Coosa County Sheriff's Office (CCSO) dispatcher called CCSO Deputy 209 with a call of shots fired on County Road 14. The deputy, CEO Hayes, and myself responded. Drake arrived on the scene and immediately called and told me he had located a dead deer near the county road on the Brown estate property. Examination revealed the three-point buck had been shot. The deer was within 150 feet of the Brown residence. It was limber and warm indicating it had only been dead a short time as it was a cold night. Drake took up a position where he could observe the deer in the event the shooter returned to retrieve it. He called the deputy and explained the situation to him and asked that he stay out of the area in case the shooter came back.

Drake contacted the complainant, who reported she and her husband had heard a shot and had observed a vehicle traveling east on County Road 14. He advised her he was in the area and would handle things if the shooter returned.

Knowing the area well, I decided to take up a position on County Road 18 at Rehobeth Church approximately one-half mile from County Road 14, and about three-quarters of a mile from where the deer was shot. As I settled in, I could not help but remember a call many years earlier. Night hunting was rampant and on the rare occasion that I wasn't out working, I was monitoring the police scanner at my house in case yet another night hunting call came in. About 10 p.m. the scanner came to life; however, it wasn't the sheriff office dispatcher as usual, it was CEO Earl Brown. I could tell by his voice he was highly irritated and what he said next helped me to understand why. He reported someone had just shot a hog in his pasture and he was out with the two culprits! I immediately grabbed my gun belt and ran for my truck. I knew Earl would be some more upset, so I thought it would be a good idea to get there as quickly as possible.

After a really quick trip, I arrived on the scene. Earl had everything in hand; however, he was fit to be tied. He quickly told me those blankety-blanks had shot his domestic hog in his pasture. I looked at the two men and could easily see they knew they had messed up big time. The two violators paid fines, costs and restitution totaling more than $4,200! As I was thinking back on that event, my reminiscing was cut short by a gunshot off to the west.

As I started my truck and headed toward the shot, Drake came over the radio asking if I had heard the shot. I advised him it was just west of me and I was headed toward it. Less than ten seconds later, I topped a hill at the intersection of Little Road and County Road 18 and saw the illumination of the lights of a vehicle coming toward me. I pulled to the side of the road and turned my lights off. Seconds later a truck came into view. Well, I should say its lights came into view seeing how that was all I could see. In addition to the headlights, the vehicle had two LED light bars and two more LED lights mounted on the front of the truck. All of the lights were illuminated and the volume of light they put out was such that I could not see the truck at all.

I allowed the truck to pass me and I immediately pulled out behind the vehicle, a black Ford truck with an Elmore County tag. Elmore was the county directly south of ours and we were only about five miles from the county line. I activated my blue lights and the vehicle pulled to the side of the road. I called the sheriff's dispatcher and told them I was stopping a vehicle and gave them the tag and location. When I saw the Elmore County tag, it brought to mind a recent correspondence with CEO Sgt. Keith Mann, the Macon County game warden. He had reported a group of kids from Elmore County were night hunting regularly in his area.

I approached the vehicle, an extended-cab pickup, and immediately noticed a male in the driver's seat and a female in the back seat. I gave the loud verbal command for both occupants to put their hands up. As I eased up to the driver's door, I asked if they had a gun and the driver replied they did not. I told them to keep their hands up where I could see them.

The fact there was not a front seat passenger in the truck immediately got my attention. Stopping a vehicle at one o'clock in the morning and finding a driver with a passenger in the back seat is what we would call a clue. Based on my experience, I felt certain the shooter had got out to retrieve a deer. I asked where the front seat passenger was and the driver stated they did not have one. I opened the door and got the driver out and placed him on the side of the truck. I patted him down for weapons and again asked if he had a weapon and he again stated they did not have one.

As I hope you can imagine, I was on high alert and not in a mood to mess around. The next words to come out of the driver's mouth did not help things. I again asked where his passenger was and he replied that a guy he did not know had told him to get in the truck and drive it. Let's think about that statement for a moment which is something I do not think he did. I guess he wanted me to believe he was just standing alongside the road at one in the morning and a guy came driving along, got out of his truck, and forced him to get in it and drive it. While I've witnessed a lot of crazy things in the middle of the night in the middle of nowhere, that hasn't been one of them.

I could hear what I felt sure was Drake approaching our location at a high rate of speed. I felt like he needed to go back down the road to where I thought the shot was and see if he could locate someone there. However, I wanted some more information before he went down there. I had the driver pressed against the side of the truck when Drake pulled up. Seeing how the fellow wasn't being very truthful, I decided to try another tactic. I told both subjects to listen to me and I recited the Miranda warning to them. Over time I had learned when you read the majority of people their rights, they automatically assume they are on their way to jail. While that is usually not the case, they still believe it. While some suspects will clam up after being read their rights, others decide they might can help themselves by cooperating.

I finished with the rights and asked the driver if he was going to tell me who was with him or not. He took the path that many use. He began trying to distance himself from what was going on and began to put it on "they." He said, "They weren't shooting at a deer, they were just shooting into the air." I responded, "If they just shot into the air, why did they get out of the truck?" He said he did not know but they had told him to let them out and for him to drive off.

I turned to Drake and told him there were at least two people on the ground and they were likely armed. I told him I believed the shot was near the Tar Bucket Road. He took off headed to that location. I told the driver to stay on the side of the truck and I moved to the cab of the truck. I reminded the female passenger in the back seat to keep her hands up where I could see them.

As I shined my flashlight in the front floorboard of the truck, I spotted a rifle barrel. I reached and got the barrel and was surprised to find that was all it was, a barrel. I moved to the passenger side of the truck and opened the door. I asked the young girl in the back seat if there were any firearms in the truck and she said she did not know. I shined my light into the rear floorboard and saw what appeared to be the end of a gun barrel. I removed a blanket from the back floorboard, which revealed a break action rifle. I removed the gun from the truck. I opened the action and found the .243 Winchester was loaded. I took the gun and secured it in my vehicle.

5

I moved back to the two suspects and asked them for their driver's licenses. I advised them, in a tone I felt would get their attention, that my partner was about to encounter whoever had been in their vehicle and I wanted to know whether or not that person had a gun. The driver said he did not think they had a gun but there were two people. The young man told me he was just the driver and he had nothing to do with what had occurred. I did not take the time to explain he was up to his neck in this.

The driver was twenty-one-year-old Barry Lackey and the passenger was his nineteen-year-old girlfriend, Deb Marks. Officer Hayes called me and stated he had not found anyone along the road. Lackey overheard the radio traffic and stated he thought he could get the individuals to come out. I asked if he could call the individuals. He said yes, but then his girlfriend said both of the boys' phones had been left in the truck when they got out. I decided to move back to where the shot had been fired. I told the driver to go back to where the fellows had got out of the vehicle.

I followed the pair to the site, which was only a couple hundred yards from the end of the Tar Bucket Road. Lackey got out and attempted to coax the other two individuals out of the woods. Drake returned to our location and began looking for the deer. I asked Lackey for the identity of the other two people and he identified them as eighteen-year-old Billy Box, who was the owner of the truck, and nineteen-year-old Trevor Green, who he said was the front-seat passenger and shooter. Calling their names over my truck public address system repeatedly yielded no response.

Drake returned from the woods and stated he had not found anything. I asked Lackey if he was sure this was the right spot and he stated it was and stated the deer had been standing behind the barbed wire fence on the property. This was the first time he admitted they were shooting at a deer.

Drake and I stepped off to the side and tried to figure out just where we were in this situation. It was obvious the group had shot at a deer. We felt it was a good bet they thought they had hit it or they would not have gotten out of the truck. We assumed they had spotted either Drake or all of us and had either hid in the woods or had taken off. If all of that was true, we still weren't sure of what our next moves were. We knew if we did not find the other two individuals it would be difficult to tie them into the situation. Not impossible, but difficult. We decided we needed to get as much info as we could from the two folks we did have. I told Drake we would question them and see where it went from there.

We returned to the truck where the girl was still sitting in the back seat and asked her if there was anything illegal in the truck. She gave the customary answer of "Not that I know of." Looking in the back seat, I noticed a zippered bag and asked her what it contained. She said it was "diabetic stuff" that belonged to the truck owner, Box. She said the young man had recently had a $20,000 insulin pump implanted in his body and had a monitor on his arm. She said he was a very bad diabetic. This changed the complexion of things. I told Drake I felt we needed to contact Lt. Fincher and let him know what we had going on. As I walked away to call the lieutenant, Barry Lackey approached me. He said he really didn't need to get into trouble because he was on probation for doing this same thing last year. Things were changing by the minute. Lackey went on to say if he got in trouble again he would have to serve sixty days in the Macon County jail. That was some interesting information. Once again, I remembered what Keith had reported and made a mental note to get in touch with him.

I contacted Lt. Fincher and advised him of the situation and told him I felt we needed to contact Box's parents and get them en route. Although the young man had left the scene of his own volition, I knew if my eighteen-year-old severely diabetic son was possibly lost somewhere in some woods he wasn't familiar with, I would have liked to be contacted. The lieutenant concurred and stated he would be en route to our location.

I had Lackey locate Box's phone and call his dad. Mr. Box was advised of the situation and asked to come to the scene. I gave him directions and he said he would be en route shortly. I decided we should probably do the same for our other suspect as well. I asked Lackey to locate Green's phone and contact his parents. He told me he would contact them, but I would need to talk to them. I noted this was a little different from what had just occurred. He dialed the phone and handed it to me. I informed Mr. Green of the situation and asked him to come to the scene. He said he would be en route.

Seeing how both sets of parents were located in Elmore County, and the fact it was now approaching 2:00 a.m., I knew it would be a while before they arrived. Therefore, I decided to go ahead and take a statement from Lackey. I reminded him I had already advised him of his rights and he said he understood. I used a technique I had often employed. I asked him to tell me what had occurred and to start from about two o'clock in the afternoon. I had found that most folks in this type situation had already been working on the lie they were going to tell me. However, giving them a start time they weren't expecting often derailed their train of thought.

Lackey thought for a moment and said he and the others had been fishing on Lake Martin earlier in the day. They had decided to go riding in Coosa County. He was driving with Trevor Green in the front passenger seat and Box and Marks in the backseat. He said they drove up Highway 9 and then took County Road 14 to Highway 231 and were on their way back when Green said, "Hit the brakes." He stopped the truck and Box passed Green a

8

gun from the back seat and he fired a shot out the window at a deer. Green and Box got out and told him to go down the road and then come back and get them. That was the end of his statement. I felt certain he had omitted a few details. While I couldn't be sure, I had a strong suspicion these were the same folks who had shot on County Road 14.

I moved to the truck where the young woman was seated and told her I wanted to take a statement from her. I reminded her I had advised her of her rights earlier and she said she remembered. Her statement was much shorter than the other. She claimed she had been asleep and was awakened by a gun shot. She said Green and Box got out of the truck and told Lackey to go down the road and come back and get them. I asked her how the gun got in the back floorboard. She replied, "Trevor handed it to me and I put it in the floor." This was interesting in a couple of ways. Of course, when I had asked her if there was a gun in the vehicle she had said she did not know. Obviously, that was a lie. The other thing I found interesting was when I had removed the gun from under her feet, it was loaded. In my experience, most night hunters do not take time to reload a single-shot rifle when they are jumping out of a truck to retrieve a deer and aren't taking the rifle with them. I finished taking her statement and had her sign it. I asked if she had someone who could come and pick her up and she said she did and I told her to call them and get them en route.

Lt. Fincher arrived and was apprised of the situation. Drake again searched the area and found some blood, which eventually led to a doe deer. The deer was still warm and the blood had not coagulated. We continued efforts to call the men from the woods to no avail.

Mr. Box soon arrived and was informed about what all had transpired. We explained our concern based on his son's medical condition. CEO Hayes drove Mr. Box up and down the road with him attempting to coax his son out of the woods by calling to him on the truck's public address system. He received no answer.

Mr. and Mrs. Green arrived. They were brought up to speed on all that had occurred. Mr. Green stated he had talked to his son, Trevor, earlier. He said he had wanted him to attend a family get-together and offered to give him some gas money but Trevor had said he had already drunk several Natty Lights and would not be coming. Mr. Green went on to say he had told his son to quit doing this kind of thing. I asked if he meant he had asked him to quit night hunting and he said yes. He stated the boy had been pursued by law enforcement the previous year while night hunting and after eluding the officers had rolled a truck, totaling it. I was a little surprised the man was so forthcoming with the information. He told us he had been caught several years earlier and had told his son not to come to Coosa County and try it because the judge in Coosa County didn't play around! While this was interesting, it was about to get more so.

Mr. Green turned and pointed at Barry Lackey and said, "There's the problem right there!" He went onto say that Lackey was the ringleader and was the reason all of this was happening. I now understood why Lackey did not want to talk to the man on the phone earlier.

Mr. Green began calling for his son to come out. He also spoke with his other son on the phone and told me he was coming to look for the boys as well. He walked over and looked in the truck and stated a bottle of tequila inside had come from his house. I told him we needed to leave everything where it was for now.

Nearly three hours had passed and we had not had any luck in locating the two night hunters. The lieutenant, Drake, and I talked and decided we might as well turn the vehicle over to Mr. Box and allow the parents to try to find the men. A release for the truck was prepared and signed by Mr. Box. We explained to the parents we would likely be obtaining warrants on the entire group and would be in touch with them soon. Mr. Green commented all of this could have been avoided if his son would have come to the prison for the family get-together as they had planned. I felt certain there was blood trickling down my chin since I was biting my lip so hard I had lost feeling in it! This was the second time he had made that statement. However, it was the first time the lieutenant had heard him say it. Looking at his face, it was all I could do not to laugh out loud. As he looked at me I could tell he too was biting his lip and his look was asking, "Did he really just say that?" I've said this a thousand times and it's still true, you can't make this stuff up.

At approximately 5:30 a.m., we were preparing to leave when Mr. Green received a call from his elder son stating he had located the two young men and was bringing them back to the scene. When they arrived, Drake and I advised the men of their rights. I took Billy to my truck and Drake took Trevor to his and we took their statements.

Trevor was very cooperative and gave what appeared to be a complete statement. He said he and the others had decided to come to Coosa County and try to shoot some deer. They discussed whether to use the .22-caliber barrel or the .243 barrel on the gun and although he thought they should use the .22 because it was quieter, they put the .243 barrel on the gun, which belonged to Box. He said they saw a deer on County Road 14 and Lackey shot it. They went on down the road and crossed Highway 231 and went to where a friend of his had some land. They came back to 231 and turned onto County Road 40 and then to County Road 18 where they spotted a deer and he shot it. He and Box got out to get the deer and Lackey drove off. They did not find the deer. They started seeing trucks on the road and got scared and moved

11

out of the area. Eventually Box's blood sugar began to drop and they started trying to find help. Later his brother, Rhett, picked them up.

Knowing both Lackey and Marks had left the shooting of the first deer out of their stories, I asked Green to elaborate on the first deer. He did not hesitate. He said Lackey was driving and spotted the deer. He took the rifle and shot the deer. I thanked him and told him I would talk with him again shortly.

Green's statement not only implicated Lackey in shooting the first deer, it also blew a hole in the girl's statement seeing how if they had already shot one deer, I didn't think she was actually awakened by the second shot as she had claimed.

I conferred with Drake and read Box's statement. It was almost identical to the one I had received from Green. He also had stated Lackey had shot the first deer. While we were taking the statements, a family member of Deb Marks had arrived to pick her up. We made sure we had good contact information for everyone involved and explained to them how the process would go. They were all allowed to leave. The sun was now up and we headed home for a little, very little, sleep.

The next morning, I sat down and wrote out everything that had occurred and began thinking about all the possible charges. There were a lot of them. Since there were two incidents, it would be legitimate to charge them with both. This would mean there could be two charges for hunting at night, hunting from a public road, hunting without a permit, and hunting by aid of a vehicle. In addition, since the deer was shot fifty yards from the house on the Brown estate, the charge of hunting within one hundred yards of a dwelling would apply as well. Furthermore, Lackey would be given a traffic ticket for driving the vehicle with the light bars illuminated.

As you can imagine, that was a lot of paperwork.

I contacted Sgt. Keith Mann, the Macon County game warden, and let him know we had apprehended the group. He verified they were some of the folks he had been after. He said what the suspect had told me concerning him being on probation and possibly having to serve sixty days in jail if convicted was true. I told him we would keep in touch and let him know how it went.

We met with the circuit clerk and laid out our case. We decided to charge each individual with one case of hunting at night, without permit, from the road and from the vehicle. The driver, who shot the first deer, would also be charged with hunting too close to a dwelling and the driving offense. The summons, seventeen of them, were prepared.

We contacted the defendants and instructed them to meet us at the Coosa County jail on Saturday afternoon. All of the defendants showed up. We explained the process advising them of their court date and the consequences if they decided not to show up. In addition to the summons, I issued the driver a written warning for driving with the unauthorized lights.

The court date arrived and we learned that all but one of the defendants had acquired attorneys and had their cases continued. However, Mr. Green appeared. The judge asked if he wanted to have an attorney appointed to represent him and he declined the offer. We had previously talked with our assistant district attorney (ADA) and had told him if the subjects wanted to plead guilty we would drop the hunting without a permit case. The judge read the charges and asked how he pled. The young man said he pled guilty. The ADA then informed the judge that we would drop the permit charge. The judge calculated the fines and court costs and informed the defendant the total came to $4,100. In addition, he would be sentenced to thirty days in jail on each charge which would be suspended on payment of the fines and costs and his hunting privileges would be suspended for three years. Things had proceeded smoothly up to this point. However, the wheels were about to come off.

The judge looked at the young man and asked when he thought he could pay the fines and costs and he responded, "I don't know." While it was probably an honest answer, the tone sounded a little belligerent. The judge did not appreciate that. He asked the question again and received the same answer. The judge then told the defendant it was obvious he needed some time to think about things and he had just the place for him to do that. He told the bailiff to take the man to jail. The man was escorted out of the courtroom.

Eventually the judge took a recess. The parents of the defendant immediately started trying to get our attention. We went over and spoke with them. They of course wanted to know why the judge had put their boy in jail after he had pled guilty. I told them the judge was the one who knew the answer to that; however, I felt their son didn't understand what the judge was looking for when he asked him when he would be able to pay the fines and costs. When he had replied "he didn't know" I felt the judge thought he was being flippant and did not appreciate it. The parents asked the question they really wanted an answer to and that was "How do we get him out?" I told them I would talk with the ADA and see if we could not get the defendant back before the judge, but he would need to be ready with his answers of how much he could pay today and when he would have all of it paid.

I got in line to speak with the ADA. On district court days the ADA is a busy person. Every attorney and half the officers in the courtroom need to speak with them at one time or another. I spoke with him and explained the situation. He said he would bring the case back before the judge.

When court resumed, the judge picked up where he had left off on the docket. When there was finally a break, the ADA approached the bench and asked the judge to revisit the Green case. Trevor was retrieved from the holding cell and brought before the judge. He was ready with the answers when the judge asked what he could pay and when he could satisfy the debt. He was released from custody.

As we waited for the next court date, something that had never happened before, happened. They called it COVID-19 and it turned out to be quite the adversary. It decimated the court process. We saw all cases continued for months. Eventually, another first occurred. We received emails advising our cases had been set for a virtual court. However, this action would also be derailed. Finally, our cases were set for court. It would be an unusual setup in that a limited number of people would be allowed in the courtroom.

Prior to the court date, I received a call from the ADA. He told me the defense attorney for Barry Lackey had made a request for discovery and I needed to send him a copy of any evidence I had pertaining to his case. He asked me to send the copies directly to the attorney. That was a first for me. About a week later, I received another call from the ADA. He said the defense attorney had some questions for me and asked if I would call him. This was another first. I told him I would call him.

I called the attorney. He asked me if we had ever met. I told him I had met both him and his father many years ago on their property in Coosa County and I had provided them with some wildlife management advice. He remembered it. We talked about hunting and this and that and I was beginning to wonder if we were going to talk about the cases. Finally, he said he had a couple of questions. His first question was what my probable cause was for stopping his client. I told him after hearing a shot from a high-powered rifle, I observed his client driving a truck on the county road with two LED light bars and two other

LED lights illuminated in addition to his headlights. He asked if I had advised his client of his rights and I advised him I had. That was basically it. He said he would see me at court whenever it got scheduled. I feared things had gone a little too smoothly; however, I knew the case was solid and I wasn't worried about it.

Months after the incident, we were in the courtroom to hear the cases. With each defendant having a different attorney, it would be a long day of negotiations. The attorney for Billy Box decided the best course of action for her client would be to apply for youthful offender status. While I am definitely not an attorney, I will attempt to provide an explanation. Youthful offender (YO) status is available to young offenders who have little or no past criminal history. While it does not absolve them of what they did, it does keep the offenses off of their adult record. The status has to be granted by the judge and that isn't always done.

The judge granted the motion. As I said, it keeps things off the record; however, they are still responsible for paying the fines and costs incurred. The subject was assessed fines and costs of $4,050 and was sentenced to thirty days in jail on each charge, which was suspended on payment. Another aspect of the YO status is the records are sealed. That is one reason why I am not using any of the real names in this story.

The next case was for the young girl, Deb Marks. The attorney for Ms. Marks approached Drake and me and introduced himself. He explained he had been the district court judge in a south Alabama county for twenty-five years and had recently retired. He said he was a friend to the young girl's family and had agreed to assist her in the case. He said he wanted us to know that he fully supported us and appreciated what we did. While I have heard that type of rhetoric from attorneys before, I felt the man was sincere in what he said.

The attorney told us his client had no previous record and he had filed a request for YO status for her. He asked if we could possibly dismiss some of the cases seeing how his client was asleep in the back seat and was not actually taking part in what had occurred. I told him we would be glad to work with him; however, I did not believe his client was asleep and I felt she was an active participant. He was very cordial and did not dispute what I had said. We told him we would drop the permit charge since we had done that for the other defendants. He asked if we would consider dropping another charge. As I said, he was asking, not demanding, as some attorneys tend to do. I conferred with Drake and we decided that if his client wanted to plead guilty to hunting at night, from the road, and by aid of the vehicle we would remit the fines and costs on the vehicle charge. He was agreeable to that. The final amount was $1,950.

It was obvious from the activity in the courtroom the case for the last defendant was going to be handled differently. Our first clue was when the attorney showed up with a court reporter who sat up to record the proceedings. This was not normal for a misdemeanor case. I knew from experience this normally indicated the attorney was anticipating the case being appealed to a higher court. I wasn't sure why this was happening, but I assumed it had something to do with the defendant's previous charges and I did not have a good feeling about it.

While it is very common to confer with the ADA during court, in my experience, when he wants you to come to his office to discuss something, that's often not good. The ADA asked Drake and me to come to his office. He began by telling us how good a job we had done with every aspect of the case. While everybody likes to hear they did a good job, this flattery did not leave me with a good feeling. He continued saying he was sure we had noticed the attorney representing our remaining defendant had

17

brought a court reporter with him. We acknowledged we had noticed that. He went on to say he had known the attorney for twenty years and he was a good and thorough lawyer. I was getting ready to ask him to cut to the chase, but decided it was best to let him proceed at his own pace. He explained the attorney had informed him he felt his client would be found guilty and in the event that happened he was going to appeal the cases to circuit court. I just looked at him and shrugged my shoulders as if to say, "So what." He quickly said he felt certain, based on our good work, we would prevail in circuit court as well. Although I had an idea, I was wondering what the deal was. I was about to find out.

The ADA took a deep breath and said, "Here's the situation." The defense attorney had shared with him his client had been convicted of hunting at night in Macon County the previous year and was on probation. He said one condition of his probation was he not be convicted of any violations and if he was he would have to serve sixty days in the Macon County jail. He went on to say the attorney was deeply worried his client would not survive in the jail. His reason for believing this was his client was a small-in-stature white kid and the inmates in the Macon County jail were almost 100 percent black. I was thinking to myself since the boy had told me the night of the incident that he would have to go to jail in Macon County if he got in trouble, he knew full well the chance he was taking by night hunting. The very offense he was on probation for. I held my tongue.

The ADA continued and said the attorney was pleading for help and had offered for his client to pay the maximum fine in each case if the cases could be placed on the administrative docket. The admin docket was in effect a pretrial diversion plan. The defendant would pay the fines and costs and would be placed on probation for a specified period. If he had no violations during the probation period, the charges would be dismissed. As I have written in the past, I wasn't a big fan of such "plans."

I'm sure the ADA could see the disappointment on my face. He told us he knew this wasn't the result we had hoped for and he understood our point of view but he felt the defendant was in a very bad situation. I added, "Of his own making," and he immediately said no one was disputing that. Seeing how I was leaning, the ADA moved forward. He said if we did not accept the deal, then the cases would be continued to circuit court. He told us that due to COVID-19, our circuit court was backed up significantly. He explained we had at least six homicide cases that were slated for circuit court. Unfortunately, in our small county, we normally have trial court only once or twice a year. Therefore, it would likely be two years before our cases would be heard. He reiterated he would be happy to go in whatever direction we wanted to go. I asked if he would allow Drake and me to talk it over for a minute. He said sure and left the room.

I looked at Drake and asked him what he thought. He said he felt the boy deserved to go to jail but he understood where the attorney was coming from. He said he wasn't worried about the case being put off for a couple of years. I told him I agreed the defendant probably should be placed in jail; however, I could understand their point. I told him the delay did not bother me; however, my track record with circuit court had not been good. It wasn't that I had lost the cases that had been appealed. What had happened in almost every case was the circuit judge would tell the ADA he didn't want to hear a misdemeanor case mixed in with the felony cases that were being heard and to settle the case. This usually meant we either dropped one of the charges or reduced the fine. Knowing that, I did not know whether it was worth waiting for the appeal to come up or not. We discussed the possibilities and decided we would accept the plea deal with the maximum fines and two years of probation.

We left the office and found the ADA and told him we would agree to the plea agreement. He thanked us and said he thought it would be the best way to go. We told him we had dropped the hunting without a permit charge on the other three defendants and it would probably be fair to do that in this instance as well. We returned to the courtroom and the ADA advised the defense attorney of the decision.

It took a little while for the attorneys to work out the details. Eventually, the ADA approached the judge's bench and told him we had reached an agreement. Mr. Lackey would be pleading guilty to hunting at night and would pay a fine of $2,000 plus court costs. He would plead guilty to hunting from a public road and would pay a $1,000 fine plus court costs. He would plead guilty to hunting by the aid of a vehicle and would pay a fine of $500 plus court costs. He would plead guilty to hunting too close to a dwelling and would pay a fine of $500 plus court costs. Each case carried with it thirty days of jail time which was suspended on the payment of the fines and costs. Mr. Lackey would be placed on twenty-four months of unsupervised probation during which time his hunting privileges were revoked. The ADA made it exceedingly clear that if the young man failed to pay his fines and costs or was charged with any violation during the two-year period, the agreement would be voided and he would again face the charges. If, he was in compliance after two years, the charges would be dismissed. After all was said and done, Mr. Lackey's fines and costs amounted to $5,400.

The total fines and costs in this incident were $15,500. I do not know exactly how much the defendants paid in attorney fees; however, I think it would likely total between $5,000 and $10,000. If you are like me you are thinking that's a lot of money.

However, there is something else that we need to think about. The first shot fired was at a deer standing within fifty yards of a house. The second shot was fired on a lot that was set up for a mobile home and where there had been a mobile home previously. Both of these shots fired indiscriminately from a high-powered rifle into the darkness could have easily killed someone. This happens many times each year.

You may have asked yourself why someone who knows serving sixty days in jail hangs in the balance would be willing to commit the same crime again. That's a good question. Knowing there are severe consequences will make many folks think twice before acting. Something I have heard repeated many times is, "It's only illegal if you get caught." While I believe many people think that is true, it obviously is not. However, I think part of the answer of why people repeat crimes after having been caught is they do not think they will be caught again. One might think that is silly seeing how they had been caught before. However, we don't know how many times they have gotten by with the activity before. As in this case, one of the defendants' dads said he had run from the game warden the year before and, while he totaled his vehicle, I feel certain it was still a thrill to get away with the illegal activity. I am convinced that is the motivation for many game law violators. Committing the violation without getting apprehended is a rush. It's exciting. It is celebrated. The chance of the glory of success makes it worth the risk—for some.

Life is chock full of choices. The choices we make often chart the course of our life. I believe choices have consequences. As in this story, some consequences can be avoided, for a time. We would do well to remember there are consequences we will not avoid. To me, one of the most impactful verses in the Bible is Galatians 6:7. It says be not deceived, God is not mocked. You will reap what you sow. The only way we are going to get by with anything is if we seek the forgiveness and saving grace offered by Jesus. Rest assured, none of our actions go unnoticed by the Lord. We will answer for each word and deed. We can go into that day of judgment alone, or we can have the ultimate advocate. I've selected Jesus and I highly recommend Him!

Over the Limit, What Limit?

DURING THE EARLY PART OF MY CAREER the opening day of the dove season was a huge event. Thousands of folks across the state were more than ready to take to the fields after a long, hot summer. That surely isn't to say that early September was not blistering hot. That was especially true in the middle of a wide-open dusty field in central Alabama. However, the normally hot and humid weather didn't seem to deter many of the folks who were ready to do some shooting.

For the game warden, the weeks prior to the opening of dove season meant a lot of hiking in the hot weather. No, we were not just walking for fun, we were checking fields to ensure folks were playing by the rules. The primary violation committed by dove hunters was hunting over bait. Although it wasn't terribly difficult to manipulate a field in a manner so it was legal to hunt over, some folks just were not satisfied unless they added some wheat or cracked corn just to "sweeten it up," as many referred to it.

This sweetening was accomplished in many ways. While some people brazenly spread the feed with a tractor and spreader and did not try to hide it, others would go to great lengths to try to avoid detection. You would not believe to what ends people would go. When folks decided to go to extraordinary levels to hide their evil deeds it meant we had to work that much harder to reveal their bad behavior.

It is very interesting to me the effect the presence of a game warden has on various materials. Sometimes it's metal, sometimes its fiberglass, and sometimes it's organic. For whatever reason the presence of the game warden evidently makes the material immediately get hot. You can tell this is happening when you arrive and you see someone immediately drop their shotgun, throw down their fishing rod, or start tossing doves into the weeds or fish into the water. It is weird. It is an odd phenomenon; however, it occurs fairly regularly. Game wardens are taught to be alert when approaching hunters and fishermen just in case the phenomenon occurs. Another important side effect of the phenomenon is it makes some folks' feet get happy and they usually quickly begin moving in the opposite direction. This type of activity is what we refer to as a clue. When this happens, it is a good idea for the officer to check the folks out and see what's going on.

On opening day of the 2019 dove season I was working in Tallapoosa County with rookie Conservation Enforcement Officer (CEO) Ryan O'Meara and fellow special task force member CEO Jinks Altiere. Our day had been mostly uneventful with relatively few people found shooting. Late in the day we decided to check a field on Elkahatchee Road, not far out of Alexander City. I had been coaching Ryan on various things to look for when approaching a dove shoot and hoped we would have an opportunity to observe some of what we had been talking about. Ryan and I were riding together and Jinks was following us in his vehicle. The field we were approaching was about three hundred to four hundred yards off the road. Although it had a good road/driveway leading to it, I knew we would be spotted as soon as we left the county road. As we pulled off the roadway, I reminded Ryan to be aware of anyone making any furtive movements.

The setup was a disked field approximately three acres in size between the landowner's house and equipment sheds. Round bales of hay had been placed in strategic spots for folks to sit beside. My initial assessment, based on the size of the area and the number of pickup trucks present, was there might be fifteen guns on the field.

There were two driveways that led to the field. Ryan and I took the one to the north and Jinks took the southerly one. As fate would have it, our driveway went right past a round bale of hay with two shooters positioned at it. As we approached, it was as if one of the shooters at the round bale evidently decided he wanted to provide Ryan with an excellent example of what we had just been talking about. The man turned and looked at us coming up the road and immediately propped his gun against the hay bale and started walking away at a pretty fast pace. I said to Ryan, "Are you seeing that?" and he replied, "I am." I told him to check that guy first and I would get some of the others. I stopped the truck and Ryan jumped out and began pursuing the fast-walking man.

I looked back at the hay bale from where the guy had left and observed what appeared to be a young kid standing beside it. As I looked to the south there were three individuals at the next hay bale about one hundred yards away and I decided to check them first while keeping an eye on Ryan.

The trio I encountered were three young boys not old enough to need a license. When I asked to see their birds, I quickly realized we had a problem in that all three had kept their birds together in a pile. This is a common problem on dove fields. The problem is the limit for doves is an individual possession limit not a party limit. That limit is fifteen. It is not unusual to check a hunter and find they possess more doves than the limit. Often, they will say they have killed twelve and the other eight belong to their buddy who is across the field. That is a problem in that I do not know who actually killed the birds. Sometimes I can locate the buddy and they have no other birds and provide the same story and things can be sorted out. In the event the buddy can't be located, the shooter in possession of the birds is in a fix. Another common scenario is I locate said buddy and he has his own pile of birds. Even if he says he did leave a few with his friend, it is now impossible for me to know how many each one has taken. However, I can know how many each one has in possession.

Alabama Regulation 220-2-.18 reads, "It shall be unlawful to take or attempt to take or have in possession more than the daily bag limit of any game bird, game or furbearing animals."

As I dealt with my folks, I would occasionally look over at Ryan and see what was happening with him. I noticed he had returned to the hay bale with the adult in tow and appeared to be checking the shotguns to make sure they were incapable of holding more than three shells, which is the rule if you are hunting migratory birds. I moved on to the next closest hunter. I was noticing everyone I encountered seemed to have several birds. That made me wonder what was attracting the birds.

I eventually made my way into the disked field. I immediately noticed the field had wheat about four to six inches high growing sporadically across the landscape. Unfortunately, I also noticed what appeared to be fresh wheat seed in the field. The sprouted wheat and the unsprouted wheat in the same field indicated to me the field had likely been double-seeded, which is not legal to hunt over. The violation was not egregious; however, I felt it was a violation.

I conferred with Jinks and he was of the opinion the field was not far enough out of compliance to warrant ticketing everyone. We debated it and decided we would determine who had prepared the field and explain what we had observed and make sure they were aware what was and was not legal.

We located the landowner's son-in-law and explained the situation to him. We also had a couple of other combined limits we addressed with warnings. While this was going on I kept looking over at Ryan and he appeared to be busy with some paperwork of his own. We finally finished with the field and got in the truck and headed out. I was anxious to hear what the young officer had found and he was more than excited to share it. I told him not to leave out any details.

He started by saying the man walking away was indeed suspicious. He said as he pursued the man and called for him to stop, it was if he could not hear the officer at all. He had to get within arm's length before the man stopped and turned around. He asked where the man was going and he stated he was finished hunting and was going to his vehicle to leave. Ryan asked the hunter how many doves he had killed and the man replied, "I have no idea." I stopped the young officer and told him he needed to be sure he included that statement in his narrative.

He told the man he needed to accompany him back to where he had been hunting so he could check his firearm. They headed back to the hay bale and Ryan asked who the young hunter was and the man said it was his son, who was fifteen years old. Ryan asked if the gun that was propped against the hay bale belonged to the man and he said it did. Ryan retrieved the gun and found that it was not plugged, meaning it was capable of holding more than three shells. He went ahead and checked the teenager's gun and it too was unplugged.

There was a five-gallon bucket beside the hay bale and Ryan said it appeared to be full of doves. He asked the man who the doves belonged to and the man replied, "Both of us." Once again, they had commingled their birds. Ryan and I had talked about this earlier in the day. I kept thinking he might start believing I had done this before if the things we had discussed all day continued to occur. Ryan looked at me with an excited look and said to guess how many birds they had. As I contemplated my response, he couldn't wait and excitedly blurted out, "Seventy-seven!" I quickly decided to have a little fun with the young officer and asked, "Did you write them a ticket?" His excited look was replaced by a bewildered look. He hesitated just a few seconds and then smiled and said, "Three of them."

Ryan explained he had written the adult a citation for exceeding the bag limit and two citations for his and his son's guns being unplugged. He asked if that was the right way to handle it and I told him I had no problem with it. It was getting dark and we headed for home.

I had told Ryan it was always a good idea to check the record of anyone you arrested to see whether or not it might be a second offense or for anything else that might show up. His check showed the fellow had several past criminal offenses but no hunting cases. I told Ryan we probably needed to be sure the judge understood this was an egregious violation in that the man and his son possessed forty-seven birds over their combined limit. I also reminded him that during his testimony it would be good to include the statement the violator had made saying he had no idea how many he had killed. I felt that statement made it blatantly obvious the man had no intention of honoring the bag limit.

The man appeared in court. The district judge advised the man of the charges against him and asked how he wanted to plead. The man replied he was guilty. The judge looked at Ryan and asked what was the fine on taking over the limit. Ryan responded by explaining to the judge that the man could have received forty-seven tickets, one for each bird over the limit. However, he did not want to burden the court with all that paperwork, but he would like to request the maximum fine of $500 for the over-limit violation and the minimum of $50 dollars on both the unplugged gun cases. The judge said that sounded good to him. The violator was fined $600 plus court costs.

Another thing I always tried to do with young officers was to critique almost everything we did. That was especially true with our court testimony. I told Ryan I felt he had done an excellent job in requesting the maximum fine. I told him in my long career, I had never got a $500 dollar fine for an over-limit on doves. He seemed pretty satisfied with that!

Unfortunately for us, Ryan decided to pursue a full-time career with the Air Guard in Montgomery. He explained to me he had loved his time at Game and Fish but with his previous time in the guard he could receive a full retirement in about ten or twelve years. I totally understood that. Of course, by that time he will only be in his forties so he may end up with a career in Game and Fish after all. I've heard they have some folks sixty and over who are still working! Of course, that's probably just a rumor.

A Multicolored Truck

MANY TIMES, I HAVE SAID some good information can make the difference between a stagnant investigation and the conviction of a game law violator. While having to dig for information is commonplace for the conservation officer, someone coming forward with some factual information sure can make life easier. I graciously accepted these pleasant gifts when they came along.

On December 20 at approximately 10:30 p.m. I received a call from CEO Lt. Jerry Fincher stating the Tallapoosa County Sheriff's Office (SO) had called in a night hunting complaint on Highway 49 South below the city of Dadeville. I told him I would respond. Although Tallapoosa County was east of Coosa County where I lived and worked, we worked wherever we were needed. This was especially true seeing how I was a member of our departmental special task force (STF). The STF was made up exclusively of officers who had retired and returned to work on a part-time basis. Although the group was sometimes referred to as the old geezers squad, the truth was the members of the STF had much more experience than most of the full-time officers and were often called on to assist with cases.

I had been working in Tallapoosa County while they did not have a full-time officer and had been helping train the new officer who had recently been assigned. I immediately called Tallapoosa County CEO Ryan O'Meara and told him I would be by and pick him up in twenty minutes. Ryan had been working for only a few months and had yet to work a night hunting case. I hoped this would be a good teaching case. I was not disappointed.

Ryan was waiting in his driveway when I arrived. That was a good sign. I have worked with many new officers and you always are looking for some gumption from them. Arriving on the scene we met Tallapoosa County SO Deputy Sgt. Al Wilson, Deputy Dillon Ray, and Mr. Terry Rollins, the complainant. After introductions, I asked Mr. Rollins to tell us what he had observed. He stated while outside feeding his dogs he heard a truck coming north on Highway 49. He noticed the truck stopped in the highway below his house. Although this is a fairly rural and dark area of the county, someone had recently built a boat storage facility across the road and had installed security lights across the front of it. Unfortunately, they had also sowed the area with rye grass. I felt certain deer were probably feeding on the bright green grass. In addition, there was a security light on a utility pole alongside the road. All of this illumination was of great benefit to anyone looking for deer to shoot. Luckily, it also allowed Mr. Rollins to get a good look at what was happening.

The witness stated that within seconds of the truck stopping, a loud rifle shot split the night. After the shot, the truck took off to the north at a high rate of speed. So far this was sounding good; however, I knew it always came down to how much detail the witness could provide. I held my breath hoping the witness had been paying attention. I was elated when Mr. Rollins described the truck as a multicolored pickup truck with big rims and a loud exhaust. When I asked what he meant by multicolored, he replied it had a dark-colored front fender and was white down the side and dark along the bottom. He said he had seen the truck traveling up and down Highway 49 in the past. Although hopeful, I did not let on as I took a deep breath and asked if he knew who the truck belonged to. He looked up and away as if he was thinking and then said, "I think it belongs to Ernie Jacks." Man, talk about some good information. This was sounding great and got even better when Sgt. Wilson said he thought that was correct and the young man lived just north of County Road 34 on the west side of the road. It had been a while since I had received that much good information on a night hunting case.

Mr. Rollins stated he had seen a large ten-point buck standing alongside the road several times. As we examined the area we noticed water oak acorns and deer hoof prints covering the ground. The fresh running hoof prints in the mud led from beneath the tree along the edge of the woods. Following them, we found the nice buck approximately forty yards from the road in the edge of the woods. Ryan and I dragged the deer back to my truck. Take it from me, it's not easy dragging a 175-pound deer through a muddy field. We loaded the deer in my truck, which also wasn't the easiest thing I had done that day. A quick examination revealed the deer had been shot low in the chest. I did not find an exit wound. I hoped the bullet would still be in the deer in the event I had to match it to a firearm.

As we followed Sgt. Wilson to the Jacks residence, I was trying to explain to Ryan what all we had already done and what to expect at the residence. I advised him if he would keep his eyes and ears open he would likely learn something.

Upon our arrival, which was around midnight, we noticed a couple of interesting things. One thing was a multicolored pickup truck that matched the description we had been given and the other was three men looking out the window of the mobile home. The sergeant went to the door and knocked. Mr. Earnest Jacks answered the door. The sergeant told him we needed to speak with Ernie. Mr. Jacks turned and told another young man, who we later learned was Bobby Lykes, to go and get Ernie.

Mr. Jacks stayed outside with us and stated Ernie was his son and he wanted to hear what was going on. I asked him how old Ernie was and he said he was nineteen. While we were waiting, Mr. Jacks said he was going to call his wife and tell her what was going on. It did not escape me that we had yet to inform him why we were there, yet he was going to call and tell his wife what was happening. This made me wonder how he knew what was going on. He called his wife and told her the sheriff was there and wanted to talk with Ernie and he added that the game wardens were there too. After he said we were there he added a phrase that really got my attention. He said, "You know what that means." I wasn't sure what that meant, but I had a suspicion that this might not be their first rodeo. We would see.

After probably five minutes, Ernie had yet to emerge from the home. I was getting impatient and asked Mr. Jacks if he could go in and get him. He went in the house and returned followed in about a minute by his son, Ernie. Mr. Jacks stated he had thought Ernie was in the shower but he was actually asleep in the bed. I was thinking it sure didn't take Ernie long to shower and go to sleep seeing how he was looking out the window when we drove up. I did not say anything; however, I did look at Ryan with a look that asked whether or not he caught that and he gently nodded his head that he had.

I advised Ernie I was conducting a night hunting investigation and I wanted to ask him some questions. I read him the Miranda warning from the card I kept in my pocket and he stated he understood. I asked if the multicolored pickup in the yard belonged to him and he replied it did. I asked if he had been driving it earlier that night and he said he had. Obviously, it was his truck and his having driven it earlier that night did not prove anything. However, we were getting to that part. I asked where he had been and he said he had gone to some friends' house on

Highway 50 and then returned. I asked who was with him and he said it was Bobby Lykes. I thought about having him ask Bobby to come out but decided against it. In the event I took a statement from Bobby it would be better if he had not heard what Ernie had said.

With the information flowing, I pressed forward. I asked if he hunted deer and he said he did but he had not had much of a chance to hunt this time. I told Ernie I had received a complaint that someone had shot a deer from the road and I had a witness who had stated the shot came from a multicolored truck, a truck "like the one Ernie Jacks drives." I asked why he thought someone would say that and he stated he didn't know. I asked if he thought his truck was pretty distinctive and he said yes.

I must admit, I was very surprised that Mr. Jacks had not made any comments. In my experience when you questioned a suspect with a parent present, they normally got right in the middle of it. Of course, we were still far from a confession and had a lot of ground to cover.

Although I knew it might bring things to a halt, I asked Ernie if he would go and get his gun. He immediately turned and went into the house and shortly came back with a bolt action .270 rifle. Ernie handed me the gun and I noted it was loaded with cartridges in the magazine. I handed the rifle to Ryan and asked him to write down the serial number. At that point, Mr. Jacks blurted out, "Wait a minute!" He then said, "That's my gun." He turned his attention to his son and asked him why he had got his gun and Ernie replied, "That's the one I hunt with." Mr. Jacks almost shouted, "No you don't, that's my gun and I have had it since I was eighteen years old." I asked Ernie if he had another gun and he said he did and I asked him if he would let me see it. I fully expected Mr. Jacks to tell the son not to bring any more guns out; however, he did not say anything.

34

While Ernie was retrieving the second gun, Mr. Jacks stated, "We are going to get to the bottom of this." I was in a bit of a quandary as to what exactly to think. The way the father had reacted about the gun made me think he was seeing the writing on the wall and realized he might be about to lose the gun he had had since childhood. However, if that was the case, I felt certain he would not have allowed the son to go and retrieve another gun, unless he was willing to forfeit it in place of his. I wasn't exactly sure what was happening. His comment that we were going to get to the bottom of this also threw me a curve ball.

Ernie came back carrying a .243 bolt action rifle. He again stated he hunted with his father's gun because he felt it was more powerful. I was thinking that Junior would rather I take his dad's gun than his. I knew we still had a long way to go. And it turned out it was further than I thought. I asked Ryan to record the serial number of the gun.

In what I considered an attempt at an alibi, Mr. Jacks made the comment that Ernie had been home all evening because he had needed him to stay there with a younger sibling while he went with another child to a football program.

I told Ernie it was possible the shot we were investigating came from the passenger side of the truck and I again asked if he had anyone with him. He again stated Bobby was with him but he was scared of guns and did not like to be around them and would not shoot one. Mr. Jacks said Bobby was special needs and Mrs. Jacks was his guardian.

At this point, Mrs. Jacks arrived and we told her we were investigating a night hunting complaint. In an effort to shake the truth out of them, I explained to the group there were several charges that could be brought and the truck and gun could be confiscated. I stated the fines and court costs would likely be several thousand dollars. I turned to Ernie and asked was there anything he wanted to tell me and he said, "No." I told them I needed to get their phone numbers since I would be getting back in touch with them. Ernie and his mother gave me their numbers. It did not escape me that at no time did Ernie deny committing the offense.

We left the residence and went down the road and met with Sgt. Wilson. He said he felt the boy had shot the deer and Ryan said he agreed. The deputy then told us the convenience store at the intersection of Highway 50 and Highway 49 had a camera that viewed Highway 49 and I might want to look at it. I had hoped to talk with him a little more; however, he got a call of a man who had been bitten by a snake and who had bit the snake in return. I swear to you that was what the dispatcher said. He left en route to the call. You can't make that kind of stuff up!

Thinking over what we had done, I realized I should have asked for Bobby's identification. On the way back to the residence, I told Ryan I didn't think there had been enough time but it could be that the mother had talked some sense into them and they might fess up when we got there.

Mrs. Jacks answered the door. I told her I would like to speak with Bobby. She explained that she was his legal guardian and that I would need to talk with her. As she was telling me that, Bobby walked up behind her. I asked, "Are you Bobby?" and he nodded his head yes. I asked if I could see his driver's license and he handed it to me. Mrs. Jacks did not object, which again made me wonder whether these guys were our culprits. I was a little surprised to see that Bobby was thirty-one years old. I said to Mrs. Jacks that she knew her son and Bobby better than I did and I gave her my card and told her to contact me if they needed to tell me anything. I told her I had retrieved the deer and would be checking it for a bullet. I also advised her I might be back with a search warrant for the guns. I let her know that if I had to go through all of that, we would likely be bringing several charges against the young men. She shrugged her shoulders and said, "He says he didn't do it." I wanted to say he didn't tell me that, but I knew that wouldn't help things. We left the scene.

We discussed the case all the way back to Ryan's house. I dropped him off and headed for home. By this time, it was two in the morning; however, I was pretty wired so I decided to go ahead and necropsy the deer in an effort to find the bullet. Since there was not a visible exit wound, I hoped the bullet was still inside. I knew if I could find the bullet and it was not destroyed, and if I could obtain the guns from the suspects and if the lab could find time to do the work, they would be able to tell us whether or not the bullet was a match to one of the guns. Even though there were several things that had to line up for that to happen, it was still worth a try. I removed the entrails and searched them for a bullet. Not finding anything, I searched the inside of the body cavity. While I felt certain the bullet with there, I was unsuccessful in finding it.

Later that morning, I called CEO O'Meara and told him I was unable to locate a bullet in the deer. Therefore, it would not be necessary to retrieve the guns from the suspects. Interestingly, O'Meara had some information for me. He had just learned he was scheduled to attend the Alabama Police Academy beginning in a couple of weeks, which would limit his involvement now and totally remove him from the actual court part of the case. While the sooner he got to and through the academy the better, I was disappointed he would not get to take part in the entire investigation.

A couple of days later, I contacted the other young officer in the county, CEO Johnny Johnson, and told him we needed to go and get a statement from our witness. Although Johnny was a new conservation officer, he had worked as a dog handler with the department of corrections for several years previously. This was also his first night hunting investigation and it was turning out to be a good one.

We met with our witness, Mr. Rollins, and took a statement from him concerning the night hunting incident. His statement was consistent with what he had told me the night the episode occurred. We explained to him that if things went the way we hoped we would be acquiring warrants on a couple of individuals and, in all likelihood, there would be a trial. I asked him if he would be willing to testify. The look on his face and his hesitation before answering made me a little more than uneasy. He looked me in the eye and said, "I will." I thanked him and told him I hoped it would not come to that. While sometimes it is not required for a witness to testify, you always need to make sure they are willing to if called upon. I understand there are valid reasons why people do not want to testify in court. However, if someone stopped in front of your house and unleashed a high-powered rifle round that could easily penetrate your wall and your body, I think you should not just let that go! Many people totally miss the fact that someone shooting from the road, especially at night, is a potentially deadly public safety hazard!

We left the residence and traveled to the Eagle store at the intersection of Highway 49 and Highway 50. I explained to the manager we were investigating a night hunting incident and would like to view their video footage from the night of the incident. She graciously allowed us to view the tape.

I contacted the SO dispatcher and ascertained the call had come into them at 9:50 p.m. Fortunately, CEO Johnson, being much younger than me, was very familiar with the video system and was able to find the period of time that we needed to view. Ironically while we were cueing up the video, a fellow entered the store and came walking toward me. He introduced himself and told me he lived about a half of a mile up the highway. He said he would like to report someone shooting a high-powered rifle very near his house a couple of nights earlier. I asked what time that had occurred and he said it was just before ten o'clock. I asked where his house was in relation to Mr. Rollins. He said it was just north of there and on the other side of the road. I told him that was the case we were currently working on. I was a little amused by the shocked look on his face. I asked if he had seen anything and he replied he had not but had just heard the shot. I told him we had a good idea who had fired the shot and hoped to arrest them soon. He left very excited.

On the video we observed a vehicle as it came south on Highway 49 and turned into the store across the road from the Eagle store. The video showed the vehicle entered the northeast corner of the parking lot at 9:48 p.m. After setting in the parking lot for fifty-five seconds the vehicle went back north on the highway at 9:49 p.m. While we were not able to positively identify the vehicle, I thought we might be able to get around that. I told Johnny we needed to take some measurements. However, as we were leaving the Eagle store, I noticed that a store across the road had numerous cameras on the front of their building. I told Johnny those cameras were pointed directly at where the vehicle in the video had stopped and turned around. I called the number that was on the front of the store. A woman answered and I identified myself and explained I was conducting an investigation and felt the footage from the cameras on her store could be helpful. She paused for a moment and then said she was sorry but the cameras were not real. That was disappointing but it had been worth a try.

Our measurements revealed the location where the deer was shot was approximately 1,100 yards or .6 of a mile from the store where the vehicle turned around. We did the math and determined it would take a vehicle traveling at forty-five miles per hour forty-eight seconds to travel .6 mile. The shot was reported at 9:50 p.m. While I knew the clock at the store and the clock at the SO were probably not totally in sync, it was very interesting how well the time meshed with the timing of the 911 call. Furthermore, while the video did not positively identify the vehicle that turned around at the store, it did show there were no other vehicles that went north on the highway immediately prior to the vehicle we had viewed or for the next four minutes after the vehicle we had viewed! I'm sure you might be thinking that is totally circumstantial evidence and you would be correct. However, I always remember what an old investigator once told me: there's a lot of people sitting on death row because of circumstantial evidence!

As we were traveling north on the highway it dawned on me that we could check the cameras at the stores at the next intersection and they might very well corroborate that there was only one vehicle on the road at that time that night. We pulled into the Texaco Station (store 19) at Highway 49 and County Road 34. We noted the station was approximately 3.3 miles north of where the deer had been shot. We recalled that the witness had stated the vehicle had left at a high rate of speed. We figured out that a vehicle traveling at the speed limit would cover that distance in about three minutes and thirty seconds.

We entered the store and introduced ourselves to the clerk. I explained to her we were conducting an investigation and if possible, we would like to view some of their video footage. The clerk was very helpful and ran the video back to the date we requested. As we began watching the video, it was obvious the angle of their camera was such that it did not pick up the traffic on the highway. I feared the video would be of little value. The clerk made the comment we probably would not be able to see anything unless they actually pulled into the parking lot. At 9:53 Ernie Jacks's multicolored truck pulled into the south end of the store parking lot. I could not believe our good fortune. In the video, Bobby Lykes exited the passenger side of the truck and entered the store. He made a purchase and they left a minute later going north on Highway 49. The timing matched perfectly with what the witness had said. We obtained a copy of the video, thanked the clerk profusely and left the store totally elated!

When we had spoken with Ernie Jacks he had stated it had been several hours since he had been driving his truck on Highway 49. His father stated his son had been at home all evening since he was watching a younger sibling while the father was at a football meeting. We now had video evidence to refute those statements. When you catch your suspects in lies, it often works to your advantage!

Putting all of our evidence together, I surmised that Ernie and Bobby had traveled south down Highway 49. They saw the deer on the side of the road. They went to Highway 50 where they pulled off the road and sat for fifty-five seconds. It was my guess they were loading their rifle. They eased back up the road and shot the deer. The deer ran off leaving them to believe they had missed it. They then drove north on Highway 49 at a high rate of speed and pulled into the store at County Road 34 three minutes later. Thinking they had missed the deer (since it ran out of sight) they went home. I told Johnny we would need to interview Ernie and Bobby and hopefully shake things loose.

I have found when you are investigating and the subjects of the investigation refuse to answer your calls or respond to your messages, they often have something to hide. Despite many calls and messages, I had been unable to talk with Ernie. Therefore, I did some digging and learned where he was employed. As a general rule, we normally try to avoid going to someone's workplace to talk with them. However, I said we avoid it, I did not say we don't do it. I made the decision to go to Ernie's workplace in an effort to talk with him.

I pulled into the recreational area where Ernie worked but did not see his vehicle anywhere. I went to the office and found no one there. As I rode through the area I spotted a couple of guys working and stopped and asked them if Ernie was around. They explained he was off that day. I thanked them and left. I did not ask them to have him call me because I did not think it would be necessary. Lo and behold, I was correct.

It wasn't long until I received a phone call from an angry Mr. Jacks. He was very upset that I had gone to his son's workplace. I told him if they would have returned my calls I would not have had to do that. I told him I needed Ernie and Bobby to meet me at the SO on January fifteenth at one o'clock.

On the fifteenth, CEO Johnny Johnson and I were waiting at the SO when I received a phone call from Ernie's mother. I took that as a bad sign. She stated Ernie had had to go to Montgomery for his job but he was on the way back and would be maybe fifteen minutes late. I told her we were waiting.

About fifteen minutes later, Mrs. Jacks, Ernie, and Bobby entered the sheriff's office lobby. I asked Mr. Lykes to come back first. There is something about having to go through the big metal jail door that seems to get a lot of people's attention. Mrs. Jacks reminded me she was his guardian and I told her I would be happy for her to sit in on the interview. After advising Bobby of his rights, I asked Bobby a series of questions. Mr. Lykes stated he did not shoot guns nor did he want to be around one. I could tell I wasn't going to get much from Mr. Lykes. I dismissed them and asked them to have Ernie to come in.

After advising him of his rights I asked Ernie a series of questions to determine a timeline of his activities on the night of the night hunting incident. He stated he and Bobby had gone to a residence on Highway 50 and had returned around 8:50 p.m. In the middle of the questioning, Ernie said he knew that Mr. Rollins had said he had seen his truck but that Mr. Rollins had been going around asking several people if they had shot the deer. He also said Mr. Rollins's neighbor had told him Mr. Rollins hadn't seen anything. This was interesting since we had not mentioned Mr. Rollins. Since he obviously knew Mr. Rollins was our witness, I asked him if there was any reason he could think of why Mr. Rollins would say he thought it was him who had shot the deer. He said he did not know any reason.

I told Ernie there were several problems with his story and I felt very confident he had committed this offense. He said he didn't do it. At that point, I showed him the picture from the store and asked if it was his truck and he said it was. I told him the picture came from a store camera and it was taken an hour after he said he was at home. He thought about it for a minute and said he had just been wrong about the time. I asked him to tell me about going to the store. He said he had left his house and went to the store and then returned home. Unsolicited he explained how he had pulled into the lot and where he had parked. Since this did not correspond with what I had viewed on the video, I asked him to draw me a diagram of how he had pulled into the store. He said he came from the north and turned right onto County Road 34 then left into the store parking lot. I countered that wasn't what the video showed. CEO Johnson told Ernie the video showed the vehicle had come from the south when it pulled into the parking lot. We let that hang in the air for a little bit.

After about thirty seconds, Johnny told Ernie the video from the Eagle store at Highways 50 and 49 showed there was only one vehicle that came north on Highway 49 for four minutes prior to his pulling into the store.

Unsolicited Ernie stated he was having brake trouble with his truck and it did not want to stop at the Highway 50 and Highway 49 intersection. He said he had pulled off the side of the road in a dirt area just north of Highway 50 and checked his brakes. He stated he turned all the way around and went back north on Highway 49. He said that was when he pulled into the store. While this statement totally contradicted his earlier story, it fit perfectly with the actions and timeline we had developed.

I left Ernie with CEO Johnson and went to the lobby to again speak with Bobby Lykes and Mrs. Jacks. I asked Bobby if they had stopped anywhere on their way home and he said they had not. I asked if they did not stop to check the brakes or at the store and he said they did not. I asked what he would say if I told him I had a picture of him going in the store. He then admitted they had stopped to check the brakes and had stopped at the store. I asked why he had lied to start with and he said he was scared. This corroborated my earlier view that you could not believe anything he said. I wasn't sure if this lying prompted it, but Mrs. Jacks asked if she could go and get her husband and I told her she could.

I returned to CEO Johnson and our suspect. I advised Ernie I felt the evidence was enough to convict him. I told him if he wanted to tell me the truth we would work with him on the charges. CEO Johnson asked if he wanted to write out a statement and he said he did. He wrote a few lines and asked if he could speak to his father before finishing it. Although I would rather he didn't, I knew if he told me he was leaving there wasn't anything I could do about it. I asked CEO Johnson if he would go and get Mr. and Mrs. Jacks. I thought it would be best to have Mrs. Jacks to come also since Mr. Jacks had already shown himself to be a hothead.

Johnny brought Mr. and Mrs. Jacks to the interrogation room and the first thing Mr. Jacks said to Ernie was, "I better not have been lied to." I could tell by the look on Ernie's face he had lied to his dad and now felt he had to play it out to the end. Mr. Jacks informed me he was tired of this and I was cutting into his sleep time. He stated he had lawyers in his family and they would help him. I told him he should probably contact them. Although his wife was attempting to calm him down, he was having none of it. He said Mr. Rollins was lying and there were several people who may have done this. I asked why he thought Mr. Rollins would say he saw Ernie's truck and he said because he had seen it several times. He said he knew we had looked at the video camera at the store but that we didn't have a video of him pulling the trigger. I told him we didn't need one. I informed him I felt our evidence would be more than sufficient to receive a conviction. He stated his family had never had any trouble with the law. I desperately wanted to say, "Well, you've got it now," but I held my tongue.

Ernie completed his statement and left the room. Mrs. Jacks asked what if Ernie decided to tell them something had happened? I advised her to contact me if that was the case. They asked where things would go from here and I told her I would be speaking with the ADA and likely obtaining warrants on both men and would be contacting them. I advised it would be my suggestion that they would be allowed to sign their own bond. I told Mr. and Mrs. Jacks I had been doing this a long time and I felt I could guarantee them the young men would be convicted. Based on what he had said and how he had acted, I advised Mr. Jacks he should not have any contact with Mr. Rollins since Mr. Rollins was a witness in this case and any harassment of him would be considered tampering with a witness. He said he would not have any contact with him. He said he had seen Mr. Rollins but had not spoken to him. In a surprise move, he apologized for his earlier behavior and they left.

After gathering the large pile of evidence, we had amassed, we went to meet with the ADA. It was difficult for me not to refer to him as the kid that was our ADA. When you have worked as long as I have you know a lot of people and the majority of them are younger than you. That was definitely true in this case; however, it was a little more interesting than that.

When I came to Tallapoosa County, I was pleasantly surprised to learn the identity of the two ADAs in the county. Interestingly, they were a father-and-son team. The father, in his first career, was a registered forester and was the regional forester for east-central Alabama. Therefore, he and I had worked together for many years. Not only had we worked together but we had also been members of the same hunting club for a while. During that time, he brought his two young sons to hunt on the property. The oldest one was about ten or twelve years old. The fact that that "kid" was now the other ADA in the county sort of made me feel "old as dirt!" However, I was very happy to have familiar folks to work with.

Unlike most counties, Tallapoosa had two courthouses. The location in the county where a violation had taken place determined which court it would be heard in. This incident had occurred in the south end of the county and east of the river which dictated it would be placed in the Dadeville court. We went to the Dadeville courthouse only to learn that the elder ADA was out of town.

The other courthouse was located in Alexander City. Therefore, we drove the twenty miles to Alex City and met with the young ADA and laid out our evidence. He asked what charges we wanted to pursue and I told him we would be charging both men with hunting at night, hunting from a public road, hunting by the aid of a vehicle, and possibly hunting without a permit. He said he felt like we had the evidence to make those charges stick and said they would be ready to prosecute them.

Although there were two separate court systems, the ADAs and the district judge worked both places. However, unfortunately that did not mean the two court systems worked well together. I learned early on that each system wanted to handle their own cases and frowned heavily on anyone who tried to blur the lines. That meant we had to drive the twenty miles back to the Dadeville courthouse and obtain our warrants. It surely seemed unnecessary to me; however, I had learned early on that things went a lot smoother if you didn't rub the courthouse folks the wrong way. We obtained the warrants with no problems.

Based on our past experience, I decided to contact Mrs. Jacks and ask her to have both of the men to meet us at the jail. I told her if they came and met me at the designated time, they would be allowed to sign their own bonds and would be free to go. If I had to go and find them, they would be placed in jail. She assured me she would have them at the jail at the assigned time.

We met the men at the jail. After informing them what they were being charged with, we explained their bonds were not a plea of guilt but were basically a promise to appear. However, if they failed to appear the judge could order the bonds forfeited and would issue a warrant for their arrest. They stated they understood and would be there. We allowed them to sign the bonds, which were for almost $5,000. There court date was set for early March.

No matter how thorough your investigation or how much evidence you have, there are no guarantees in the courtroom. I have seen cases I would describe as ironclad get tossed out and those that were as weak as a dishrag result in a quick conviction. You just never knew. While I felt really good about these cases, I was still a little antsy.

The March court date rolled around and the defendants and both parents were in the courtroom. The court was run somewhat loosely with lawyers and officers moving in and out. I got a copy of the docket and saw we were about in the middle, which likely indicated it would be a while before our cases would be heard. We were in a jury room located just off the courtroom when an attorney stuck his head in the door and asked if we were there for the Jacks' case. I told him we were. He stepped in and said he guessed he would be representing the two defendants. I had met a lot of attorneys in my time; however, it had been very few of them that did not seem sure whether they were representing a defendant or not. He introduced himself and said the Jacks were distant kinfolks and he wanted to see what he could do for them. I took that to mean he wasn't getting paid and that sort of explained his less-than-spirited demeanor.

He pulled out a copy of the docket and looked at the multitude of charges facing his folks. He looked at me and said, "That's a lot of charges." I responded, "They've been bad boys." I did not know whether his grin signified he wanted to make a deal or was looking forward to a fight. Before I had a chance to find out, someone stuck their head in the door and told the lawyer he was needed at the judge's bench. He left the room and I turned to CEO Johnson and CEO Jinks Altiere and said we might be there for a while.

A few minutes later the ADA came in the room and said the attorney had told him he was going to represent the defendants and he had told him just to talk with us and see if we could work something out. While I had talked with a lot of attorneys concerning cases, I didn't really trust them. I think the ADA saw that in my face and he said this was a good guy and we could trust him to do what he said. That eased my mind, a little bit.

A couple of minutes later the attorney returned and asked what we wanted to get out of the cases. I told him if they wanted to plead guilty to the other three charges we would drop the hunting without a permit. He commented that was still a lot of charges and I replied they had broken several laws. He asked whether this had occurred in our presence and I told him it had not. I told him the charges were the result of an in-depth investigation and I would be happy to lay it out for him. He said for me to just give him the high points. Although I tried not to let it show, that statement really got my attention. While I may have read more into it than what was there, I could not help but believe his statement was indicative of his lack of confidence in his clients' innocence.

I explained we had a witness who heard the shot and saw a truck that one of the defendants admitted was his sitting in the road where the shot came from. He stated the truck had taken off at a high rate of speed to the north. In three minutes the same easily identifiable truck had pulled into a convenience store three miles up the road. I told him the defendant had viewed the video and admitted it was his truck. I also told him video from two different sources showed there was no other vehicle on the road for four minutes after the incident. I noticed the look of disgust on his face was growing with each detail I offered. I told him the interviews with both subjects showed they weren't very good liars. Based on his demeanor, I had in mind what I thought might be THE piece of evidence that would get us across the goal line. I told the man I had felt certain that Ernie was going to confess during his interview; however, that was up until his dad said he had a lawyer in his family that would help get them out of this. It was blatantly obvious to even the most casual observer the lawyer did not appreciate being taken for granted. He looked at me and said, "We will see about that," and he left the room. I told Johnny and Jinks I felt like we had hit a homerun and we would know soon.

The desire to see and possibly hear the details of the lawyers' meeting with the defendants was more than I could pass up. I had to go into the courtroom and try to get a glimpse of his follow-up meeting with the family. I was not disappointed. Although my view was from across the room, the finger pointing and gesturing by the barrister was very plain. The forlorn look on the faces of ALL of the family members told me this wasn't going to go well for them. I stepped back into the jury room and awaited his return.

I was a little surprised the attorney did not return quickly. However, I realized ours were not the only cases he was handling. Attorneys often have to handle several cases on court days. Alternating between the defendants, prosecutors, officers, witnesses, and the judge is quite a juggling act.

We stepped back into the courtroom to watch the show. The courtroom was often very entertaining. I can't tell you how many court dockets I have saved because they held the notes I had written concerning things that had occurred in the courtroom. They ran the gamut from hilarious to heartbreaking.

In a few minutes the attorney approached and asked if we could talk. We went back into the jury room. He began by saying these were not bad people but the son had been a problem and he was sorry we had had to deal with it. He asked would we consider allowing them to enter into a pretrial diversion program. That wasn't something I had wanted to hear.

While many of the "programs" in the courts today are good in theory, I have seen several of them fail. In general, most of these programs are set up to give defendants a second chance. One reason I disliked the programs was that in many cases this wasn't a second chance. It was a third, fourth, or tenth chance. To be fair, I think there is some value in some "programs" in that a true first-time offender could possibly be turned around. I wish they were more successful than what I have seen.

The "program" did come with not only strings but a whole ball of twine attached. The diversion program was a written agreement between the district attorney and the offender. The contents of the agreement varied widely. Although I am far from being a lawyer, I will try and explain the program. In general, the offender pled guilty to the charges, would pay fines and court costs and the cost of the program. They would in effect be on probation for the duration of the agreement with the judge having jurisdiction over them. There was a whole laundry list of things that could be included in an agreement. In my understanding the court could insert almost anything they felt was pertinent. This might be a requirement that an offender earn their GED or that they become current on paying their child support. In the past I have requested that offenders be required to successfully complete a hunter education course. Most every program carried the requirement that offenders not break any laws for the duration of the program.

I feel certain you may be thinking there has to be a major benefit to the offender before they would enter into such an agreement. There is. In the event that the violator pays all fines and costs and fulfills all of the other stipulated requirements in the allotted time period, then the charges will be dismissed and will not show up on their record. Depending on the charge this can be a tremendous benefit. Although they seem to be few and far between, there are those who after their first brush with the law do, as they say, straighten up and fly right.

As I said earlier, I was not a fan of the "program" primarily because in my experience the participants often failed to satisfy all the requirements and we were eventually looking for them again or they were allowed to go on their way without the charges showing up on their record. However, when it was a young person, the question was did they need a criminal record before they really even started their life. I asked the attorney exactly what we were talking about. He said the two men would be pleading guilty to hunting at night, hunting from the public road, and hunting by the aid of a vehicle. This would carry with it fines and court costs totaling over $3,900 each. It also carried with it a three-year revocation of hunting privileges. I asked if they in fact would have the pay the fines and costs and he said they would. He added he hoped that would be enough to get their attention. This prompted me to ask him if they had been in this type of trouble before. While he was obviously under no obligation to answer that question, he judiciously answered, "Rumor has it." I asked for a minute to confer with my counterparts and he left the room.

I told CEO Johnson my thought was even if the charges were eventually dropped, that was a hard lick. CEO Altiere agreed. I also told CEO Johnson there would be one other stipulation that had to be met and for me it was the most satisfying. That piqued his interest, but I did not share with him what it was.

I stepped back into the courtroom. When I caught the attorney's eye, I gave him a thumbs-up and he nodded that he understood.

Whatever type of resolution that was agreed upon between the prosecution and the defense had to come before the judge and be given his blessing. As a general rule this was basically a formality; however, it did give the judge the opportunity to impress upon the defendants the seriousness of fulfilling their obligations and the consequences if they did not. There was also something else the judge often required. It was sometimes referred to as an allocution. It was the point where the defendants had to stand before the judge and the entire courtroom and admit they were in fact guilty of what they had been charged with.

As you have seen in this story, building a case is much different than making an "on-view" case. While even an on-view case takes some time to prepare, the true gist of the case is we can stand before the judge and testify we saw the defendant commit the violation. When that is not the case, bringing the charges takes a great deal of effort. Speaking frankly, many officers do not feel it is worth their time to pursue such a case. For me, there wasn't much that was more satisfying than seeing one of these cases coming to fruition. That was especially true in this case. When the father stated he had lawyers in his family and they would in effect get them out of this, I immediately vowed to myself that if that was the case, it would not be because I had not gone the extra mile.

As we stood before the judge, he asked the two young men how they pled and they did not hesitate to answer, "Guilty." It made all the time and effort worth it. I eased over to CEO Johnson and said, "That's what I'm talking about!"

I had a lot of good help in this investigation; however, it would not have happened at all if the witness had not called the SO and reported the incident. Folks, when we don't get the call, we normally do not know it occurred. Not only did this individual call, he called immediately. You saw in this story how important the timing turned out to be. If you observe a wildlife law violation, get as much information as possible and call it in right then.

I will admit that had Tallapoosa County Sheriff's Office (TCSO) Sgt. Wilson not have mentioned the video camera at the store down the road, I probably would not have thought to view it. The information it provided made me think about viewing the one from the store up the road, which turned out to be what was likely the most important piece of evidence for proving the violators' story was a lie. Living in an ultra-rural county with few stores and even fewer video cameras, I never had a store video to assist me in a Game and Fish case before this one. Ironically, a couple of years later I had an entire case caught on a Ring doorbell camera!

I was thankful I had CEOs O'Meara, Johnson, and Altiere to assist on this case. It was a tremendous teaching case. While apprehending a violator on-view is exciting, taking a little bit of evidence and turning it into multiple convictions is exhilarating. I was thankful that Ryan and Johnny were able to work through this with me. I hope they were paying attention.

The defendants standing before the judge and stating they were guilty reminded me that we will all one day be in that situation. We will kneel before Christ's throne and where we will spend eternity will hang in the balance. We will either be cast into the fiery pit or ushered through the pearly gates of heaven. Whether we are guilty or not will not be the question. The Bible says we all have sinned and come short of the glory of God. No matter how much better we may be than the next guy, we are still sinners. Remember, Jesus sees it all, just like on a videotape!

Romans 6:23 says for the wages of sin is death, but the gift of God is eternal life through Jesus Christ, our Lord. What a miraculous gift is available to us. It is only available now. When we die our fate is sealed. If we have chosen Christ as our Savior, we will spend eternity in heaven. If we haven't made that choice, we will spend eternity in hell. Today is the day of salvation. The Savior is waiting. He knows you're guilty and He stands ready to wipe the slate clean. Choose Him today and you can say, "I stand redeemed by the blood of the lamb."

I Hit That

ONE THING THAT SURPRISES many people is the fact that since we are APOST-certified law enforcement officers, we can enforce any law in the state. Of course, our primary concern is game and fish laws and regulations and we try to limit our enforcement activities to that. However, on occasion we do have to enforce other laws. We do our best to limit this to incidents where public safety is placed in jeopardy.

Working late at night gives us the opportunity to observe a lot of nefarious activity. A story a fellow officer related to me comes to mind. He was working a night hunting complaint in southwest Alabama. It was late at night when he observed a slow-moving truck coming in his direction. The driver pulled up to a gate directly in front of the officer's observation point. The fellow exited the truck and opened the gate. The truck entered the field and began shining the area with a spotlight. The light stopped moving and within seconds a shot rang out. Knowing the truck would have to come back through the gate, the officer sat tight and waited on the poacher to load the deer and come out to him.

In a few minutes he observed the headlights of the truck moving back toward the gate. As the officer watched, the driver exited the truck and moved back to the gate. With his hand on the

55

ignition switch the officer planned to let the man close the gate and then pull out on him as soon as he got back into the truck. The officer watched as the man moved to the gate. However, he did not close the gate. Instead he moved to the gate post. The officer wasn't exactly sure what was going on but he would soon find out. After hearing a few metallic noises, the fellow hoisted the gate over his head and loaded it on the back of his truck! He moved to the cab and started down the road. The officer pulled out and stopped the truck and arrested the driver for hunting at night, hunting from a vehicle, hunting without a permit, and theft of property!

While traveling on Coosa County Road 40 just south of Jacks Creek around midnight I observed a vehicle as it came up behind me at a high rate of speed. I supposed when the driver saw my light bar and LAW ENFORCEMENT written across my tailgate, they decided to back off a little bit. I went around a curve in the road and although I could see the illumination of the headlights, the vehicle never came into view. Thinking the car had possibly wrecked, I turned around and went back to check. I came around the curve and observed the car sitting in the roadway. I passed the car and turned around and came up behind the black Nissan sedan.

I stopped behind the vehicle and activated my blue lights. As I approached the running car, I observed the driver, the sole occupant of the vehicle, as he was attempting to place a beer can behind the front seat. As I observed, he spilled beer from the container in the rear floorboard. He opened his door and in a jovial tone asked, "What's going on?" I told him I was checking to see why he was sitting in the roadway. I immediately noticed the smell of alcoholic beverage was very strong. He said he had stopped to make a phone call. Scanning with my flashlight, I observed a partially filled bottle of vodka in the front floorboard. I asked to see his driver's license and he said he did not have it with him. While I was attempting to speak to him he was dialing his phone repeatedly and getting a female's voicemail. I called the sheriff's office dispatch and asked them to send a deputy to my location.

I asked if he in fact had a driver's license and he said he did not. He continued to dial his phone, calling who I would learn was his mother. I asked him to step out of the car. He switched the engine off and attempted to stand up. He was very unsteady and fell back against the car. He appeared disoriented. I asked where he lived and he pointed into the woods and said, "Right here." I advised he did not live out in the woods where he was pointing and he assured me he did. I asked what his address was and he replied, "Speed." Speed was a local community about ten miles from our current location. I told him he wasn't close to Speed and he again pointed into the woods and said, "It's right there." It was pretty obvious this guy was messed up to a point where he definitely did not need to be driving.

Coosa County Deputy Travis Ward arrived. As I spoke with the man, Deputy Ward removed a few cans of beer from the vehicle. When he removed the bottle of vodka and held it up where I could see it, the driver enthusiastically stated, "I hit that." I asked Deputy Ward if he had a portable breath tester and he stated he did and removed it from his vehicle. The suspect blew into the device and it indicated his blood alcohol content was .31. That is almost four times the amount to be considered intoxicated. The fact that the man was having difficulty standing made it obvious he was much too impaired to complete any balance-type tests. The fact he was adamant he was at his home when he in fact was ten miles from it and a mile from any house led me to believe he was too impaired to drive. As I prepared to place the man under arrest, his phone rang and it was his mother returning his call. He immediately told her she needed to come and get him. I told him that wasn't going to be possible. I asked if I could speak to her and he handed me the phone. I advised the lady her son was under arrest for DUI and he was going to be placed in the jail in Rockford. I realized this wasn't the first time she had received such a call when she immediately asked if she could come and get the car. Seeing how he had been cooperative, I told her she could. She asked me where it was and I gave her the location. She said, "Just lock it up, I've got a set of keys for it."

In the interest of the well-being of him and the public, I placed the man under arrest for driving under the influence and Deputy Ward escorted him to his car for the trip to the jail.

At the jail, the deputy told me the man had told him we had probably saved his life. The Dräger test showed his blood alcohol content level to be .33.

In addition to driving under the influence, the man's driver's license was revoked and he had an open container of alcohol in the vehicle. I chose not to arrest him for those offenses. A review of his driving record revealed he had several DUI arrests in the past. Hence his mother having the extra set of keys!

The next month he appeared in court and pled guilty to DUI. Once again, I felt as though I likely saved his life and possibly the lives of others by getting him off the road. You never knew what you might find in the middle of nowhere at midnight.

A Well-Planned Night Hunt

ON OCTOBER 15, opening day of the bow and arrow deer season, Coosa County Conservation Enforcement Officer Drake Hayes received a call concerning a large white-tailed buck that had been killed illegally. The unknown informant stated that B. J. Jones had killed the buck the night before opening day while the deer was eating at a pile of corn under a security light in his back yard. The officer asked how the caller knew this and he replied Mr. Jones had been saying he was going to kill the deer before anyone else got a chance to. He also stated someone had texted him a picture of the deer and he sent it to the officer.

Drake called me and explained the information he had and asked if I would accompany him to question the suspect. Seeing how investigations of this type were one of my favorite things, I jumped at the chance. Although our information was that Mr. Jones lived in the Weogufka area of Coosa County, the address on his driver's license was in the south end of Talladega County.

As I mentioned, I enjoyed conducting investigations. While it normally took a lot of time and effort, it was very rewarding when things came together. Many years earlier while working a break-in on the Coosa Wildlife Management Area with Coosa County Sheriff's Investigator David Windsor, he explained to me that your best bet to catch a criminal was to get on the case as quickly as possible and stay on it until you had solved it. While that wasn't always possible, I found it to be good advice. David, a brother in Christ, passed away several years ago. As I've gone through my career, I realize he taught me a good bit. I remember him telling me that when you are conducting an investigation there is no such thing as a coincidence. I have found that to be pretty accurate. I look forward to seeing David again one day and thanking him for sharing his vast experience with me.

Any time you plan to question/interrogate a suspect, if at all possible, you must first do your homework. I have always found it helpful to review the elements of the crimes that you anticipate charging the individual with. In addition, you need to anticipate the many defenses the suspect may try to employ and be ready to dismantle those attempts.

Drake and I had checked to see if Mr. Jones had his hunting licenses, including a bait privilege license, and to see if he had reported the deer harvest as required by law. The law gives a hunter forty-eight hours to report the harvest. However, the deer must be recorded either on their phone app or on a paper harvest record prior to moving the animal. Therefore, since the deer had supposedly been killed that morning, even if he had yet to report the harvest he was not yet in violation as long as he had recorded the harvest. Our check revealed that Mr. Jones had indeed reported the ten-point buck had been killed that morning at 6:30 a.m.

Drake and I went to the address on the license and immediately recognized the vehicle in the driveway as the one we had seen in the picture Drake had received. We exited our vehicle and headed toward the house. As I walked by the pickup truck, I looked in the bed and recognized the trash that was in the truck was the same as in the picture we had seen. We stepped up on the porch and knocked on the door. A middle-aged man came to the door. We told him we were looking for B. J. A young man came to the door and identified himself as B. J. He was a big boy in his early twenties. We told him we needed to talk with him and asked if he would accompany us to our truck.

Drake sat in the driver's seat with Mr. Jones in the passenger side and I was in the back seat. The officer began by telling the young man we wanted to talk with him about the deer he had killed but that it was our policy to first advise him of his rights. Drake read him the Miranda warning. B. J. stated he understood. Drake asked him to describe the hunt for us.

The young man did not seem nervous at all. He began by telling us he had been feeding corn in his back yard for over a month. He said the deer had been coming and eating there every day. Knowing several people hunted in the area, he said he knew he needed to try and kill the deer as soon as the season opened. He said he had gotten up at six o'clock and was sitting on his porch just before daylight waiting on the deer to arrive. As soon as it was good shooting light the deer came in to the corn pile that was about thirty yards away. At six thirty he shot it with a borrowed crossbow. Drake asked where he had struck the deer and he said he hit it behind the right shoulder. He said the deer only ran about thirty yards before falling.

Everything sounded feasible. Of course, it was pretty much what we had anticipated hearing. Drake asked the young man if he had gone to work after killing the deer and he said he had. He asked what time he had arrived at work and he said it was around twenty or thirty minutes after seven. When asked what he had done with the deer he said he had cut the head off and put it in the freezer and had given the deer to a fellow he worked with. We asked if he had filled out a donation form when he gave the man the deer and he said he had not. He went on to say he did not know he needed to do that. Drake explained that anytime someone possessed a harvested deer they had not personally taken, they needed a donation certificate to show who had killed the deer. He again said he was not aware of that requirement.

Everything was sounding legitimate and I was beginning to question whether our information had been incorrect or if he had just worked extra hard on developing a believable story. I was about to get my answer. Drake asked if he had taken any pictures of the deer and he said he had and quickly retrieved his phone, located the photos, and showed them to us. They were the usual pictures of a fellow with a good deer. Once again, it seemed everything was in place. Almost everything.

Drake asked if that was all the pictures he had and he stated it was. It was now time to drop the hammer. Drake retrieved his phone and pulled up the picture we had. He showed it to Mr. Jones and asked, "Is this the same deer?" The fellow looked at the picture for a few seconds. He then looked at the floorboard of the truck. While staring at a spot in the floorboard, he said, "I shot the deer at ten o'clock last night." We asked did he really shoot it with the crossbow and he said he had. We asked where his crossbow was and he said he had borrowed it from a friend and had already returned it.

Drake advised him we would be obtaining warrants for hunting at night and hunting in closed season. He also told him we would be confiscating the head and antlers. The man said the head was in the freezer in the house. While Drake escorted him to the house to retrieve the deer head, I took pictures of the bed of the truck. As we drove away, I looked at Drake and said, "That's what I'm talking about!" I told Drake he had done a masterful job of questioning the man and obtaining the confession.

Three months later, Mr. Jones appeared in district court and pled guilty to his charges. He paid over $2,500 in fines and court costs and lost his hunting privileges for three years. The confiscated deer head and antlers were given to the Department of Conservation to be displayed in our violator trailer. The violator trailer is set up at various gatherings to emphasize that poachers are stealing these trophies from law-abiding hunters. If you know of someone who is stealing wildlife, report them. This case would not have been made without someone caring enough to contact us. If you see something, say something.

A Poor Judge of Distance

As a general rule, most of our cases are situations concerning humans versus wildlife. However, we dealt with several hunter-versus-hunter problems and a few hunter-versus-non-hunter problems. Sometimes it was difficult to know what role some of the folks involved were playing.

Conservation Enforcement Officer (CEO) Drake Hayes contacted me and informed me he had an interesting situation developing and wanted to know if I could assist him. He had been contacted by both parties of a hunting-without-a-permit situation. Normally that would mean that someone had been hunting on a property that belonged to someone else who did not want anyone hunting on their property. However, every once in a while, we had someone who didn't want someone hunting on someone else's property. If you aren't confused yet, you likely will be shortly!

Drake stated that the land involved was previously in the Coosa Wildlife Management Area (WMA) and he hoped I could shed some light on the situation seeing how I had been working on the WMA for over thirty-three years. I told him I would be glad to help.

The first call that came in was from a young member of a local hunting club, Mr. Dennis Peppers. Mr. Peppers gave a troubling account of an encounter he had experienced the day before. He stated he and his girlfriend, Lee, were going into the woods en

64

route to their deer stands early in the morning when they met another club member who cautioned them that a nearby landowner had located Mr. Peppers's tree stand and had been trying to catch him in it. Knowing his stand was well within the boundaries of the club property, he did not think too much about it. He escorted his girlfriend to her stand and then proceeded to his.

After climbing a tree with his climbing stand, Mr. Peppers saw two men standing near the property line. He watched as one of the men, who he would learn was James Dye, approached his stand with a pistol in his hand. The other man, who was armed with a high-powered rifle, stayed at the property line. Mr. Dye told Mr. Peppers he was hunting in a safety zone and he needed to come down. Mr. Peppers told him he was on the hunting club property and not in a safety zone. Mr. Dye then told him to come down the %&*# tree and fired a round from the handgun into the ground. The other man, John Erickson, who had earlier remained at the property line, then walked over to where the other two men were.

Mr. Peppers came down the tree and Mr. Dye again told him he was hunting in a safety zone. The young hunter told the landowner he did not know what he meant when he referred to the area as a safety zone. Mr. Dye explained there was a safety zone around his property and no one could hunt there. Mr. Peppers countered that the safety zone had been in place when the property was in the state WMA; however, it was no longer designated as such since the land was now leased by the hunting club. Mr. Dye said he felt it was still in effect. He walked the young hunter about one hundred yards and showed him a safety zone sign. Mr. Peppers countered that the sign was still a hundred yards from Mr. Dye's property line. Mr. Dye told him he and his friend hunted the area and he did not want anyone to get hurt so the club members needed to stay away from his property. To emphasize his point, he told the young man to ask the last guys he had caught over there about being face down in the dirt with a 9 mm to their head. Then as an exclamation point, Mr. Dye stated he had been to prison and wasn't afraid to go back!

Mr. Peppers's girlfriend, Lee, was hunting nearby and observed the entire incident. She stated the man with the pistol was wearing a blue plaid shirt and the man with the rifle was wearing what she described as hunting clothes. She stated she had heard a shot and then saw Mr. Dennis descend the tree and walk through the woods with the men before returning to the tree stand site. She said after the encounter they went to an area with phone service and contacted the president and vice president of the club and informed them of what had occurred.

The club officers called the Coosa County Sheriff's Office and Deputy Mike Rudd responded and spoke with the club members. He also went and spoke with the landowner.

The next day CEO Drake Hayes received a call from Mr. Dye saying he wished to speak with him about an incident that occurred the previous day. CEO Hayes and I met with and interviewed Mr. Dye. He told us he owned fifteen acres he purchased twenty-one months earlier. He explained he had been having trouble with people cutting the locks off of his gate and driving on his private road. He stated the property adjacent to his had been in a safety zone when he purchased it. He said he had not learned that it was no longer in a safety zone until he had viewed a current map online and saw that the land was no longer in the management area.

He stated that a couple of days earlier at five fifteen in the morning someone came down his driveway and immediately came back out. He surmised that whoever had driven up his driveway had let someone out and they would be hunting from the stand he had located earlier in the "safety zone." Therefore, he and his friend, John Erikson, decided to go and confront the hunter. He explained the man was twenty yards across the property line in a climbing stand and was looking straight into his property. Mr. Dye said he and John confronted the young man and he explained to him he was hunting in a safety zone and too close to his property. He told the man about his locks being cut, finding trash on his property, and seeing ATVs on his property. He said he gave him his cell phone number and told him to have the club president to call him.

We walked to the property line and viewed the gate he said the locks had been cut from. We then walked the property line and Mr. Dye pointed out the area where the hunter had been up in the tree. While he did not walk over to it, he pointed out the tree that was about fifty yards across the line. We did not comment on it being twice as far as he had initially said. He stated one of his young children had told him about the stand being there.

Obviously, his story was somewhat different than the one Drake had heard the previous day. CEO Hayes advised Mr. Dye we wanted to ask him some questions and therefore he needed to advise him of his rights. He read him the Miranda warning and he said he understood. Although some of our questions had already been answered by the man while he was telling his story, we needed to get a few things on the record after he had been advised of his rights.

Drake asked if Mr. Dye and Mr. Erikson had gone to the tree stand across the firebreak on the Kaul Timber Company land. He said he had and "if that was wrong, then I was wrong." CEO Hayes asked if he possessed a pistol during the encounter and he stated he did not. Hayes told him the hunter had said he had fired a handgun into the ground when he had refused to come down out of the tree. He replied, "That did not happen." He did add that Mr. Erikson did have a .308 hunting rifle with him but no shots were fired. CEO Hayes asked Mr. Dye when he had learned there was no longer a safety zone around his property and he replied he had found out in October which was three months prior to the incident. CEO Hayes said, "So you knew the area where the hunter was was not on your property nor in a safety zone?" He replied, "Well I do now."

I said to Mr. Dye it seemed odd to me that the hunter who was where he could legally be hunting and was confronted by him would say he had possessed a gun and fired the gun if that did not in fact happen. He repeated that it did not happen. I asked if he owned a handgun and he replied, "No." I gave him my best "I know you are lying" look and after about five seconds he said, "Yes, I do." I asked what type of gun it was and he said it was a .45-caliber Glock handgun and he thought it was a model thirty-six. He said he had owned it for several years. I asked if he had just remembered that. He did not respond. We asked if there was anything else he wanted to tell us and he said no.

Once back in our truck, we looked at each other and said, "Guilty." We then began to rehash what we had heard and to figure out our next steps. It was evident there were several things in his story that did not ring true. We decided we needed to have the young hunter to show us the actual tree he was in. In addition, we knew we needed to speak with Deputy Rudd and see if he had the same feeling we did. We also felt we needed to meet with the hunting club officers to verify their lease, discuss boundaries, and so forth.

I contacted Deputy Mike Rudd and told him we were investigating the hunting incident and I would like to meet with him and discuss his interview with Mr. Dye. I have known Mike for over thirty years. We umpired Little League baseball together which was at times more dangerous than many of the law enforcement situations we have been in together!

My talk with the deputy was very interesting. Mike revealed that Mr. Dye initially stated he was armed during the encounter. He then changed his story stating he was not armed but his companion Mr. Erikson was armed. I told Mike that was some important information. He responded by asking if I wanted a copy of the video. Although I knew all the deputies wore body cams, I had not even thought about the possibility of there being a video where Mr. Dye admitted being armed during the encounter. I told him I definitely wanted a copy of the video. I asked the deputy if he thought the man had threatened the young hunter and he did not hesitate to say yes.

We contacted the hunting club officers and set up a meeting with them. I had known both of the men for over thirty years. The pair were legitimately upset that the confrontation had occurred. They advised they had not had any problems with any neighbors until the landowner had confronted a couple of their members earlier in the year. Drake and I immediately thought back to the landowner telling the hunter about holding the people face down with a 9 mm to their head. I asked for the names of the people involved in the incident and obtained their contact info. The officers stated they did not want any trouble with anyone. They also made a comment I knew was a real possibility. They said if the landowner had encountered some other members of their club, the outcome may have been much worse. I knew that was likely the case!

I contacted club member Joey Gant and asked him to give me the details of the earlier encounter. He explained he had been on the hunting club and had driven down a road on the club that his map showed going to Coosa County Road 55. He came upon a gate which was Mr. Dye's gate. He stated he turned around and as he was leaving Mr. Dye came up behind him with a gun in his hand and yelling that he was on private property. He said Mr. Dye told him someone had stolen a T-Rex off-road vehicle from him and the person who had stolen it was driving the same type of vehicle he was driving. He said he and Mr. Dye were able to "talk things out." However, he said Mr. Dye told him there was a two-hundred-yard buffer zone around his property and if they got inside of that, he would shoot them. We were obviously starting to see a pattern emerge.

CEO Hayes contacted Mr. Peppers and ascertained a precise location where Mr. Dye and Mr. Erikson had encountered him. Drake went to the location. He found the tree which had been climbed with a tree stand. He searched the ground near the base of the tree and lo and behold, he located a spent 9 mm hull. The hull was on top of the duff layer indicating it had been there a short while. CEO Hayes measured the distance from the tree where the confrontation took place to Mr. Dye's property line. The distance which Mr. Dye had claimed was 20 yards was in actuality 265 yards! Drake and I agreed that was a pretty significant difference.

With all of our new information, we returned to the Dye property in hopes of speaking with Mr. Erickson. He was not there. However, we did obtain his phone number from Mr. Dye. We asked Mr. Dye if he would provide a written statement concerning the incident and he said he had already told us what had occurred and would not give us a written statement. We had not expected to get one.

We phoned Mr. Erikson and he stated he had been present during the encounter. We told him we would like to talk with him concerning the incident. He advised his son had the flu and he would not be coming down that weekend.

Drake and I got together and discussed what we had learned. We decided it was time to meet with our assistant district attorney, Joe

Ficquette, and present our case. We laid out the details of our case for the prosecutor. We told him the behavior of Mr. Dye, as described by multiple witnesses, was disturbing. Witnesses claimed Mr. Dye has accosted at least three individuals while armed with a handgun on property he did not own or have any permission to be on. While he stated he had done this in an effort to protect his property and family, our interviews with involved parties did not indicate any of them posed a threat to Mr. Dye or his family. We explained that Mr. Dye had stated the incident with Mr. Peppers occurred just 20 yards across the firebreak on the edge of the hunting club property when it was actually 265 yards from his property line. Consequently, we felt Mr. Dye, by his actions, which were premeditated, did in fact pose a real threat of serious physical injury by firing a shot in close proximity to Mr. Peppers.

We continued to lay out our case stating we felt the fact Mr. Erikson was armed and had stated he was there to support Mr. Dye implicated him as well. We told him we felt Mr. Dye and Mr. Erikson should be charged with violating the hunter harassment law and with menacing.

He complimented our work and said he felt we had a solid case. He said he definitely felt both men were guilty of hunter harassment. However, he felt it would be best to charge Mr. Dye with reckless endangerment and unlawful imprisonment. I must admit we had not seen the imprisonment charge coming. However, he was the prosecutor. He felt the hunter harassment charge would be the only charge for Mr. Erickson. We obtained the warrants.

We contacted both men and informed them we had warrants for their arrests and needed them to meet us at the jail. We told Mr. Dye he would be placed in jail on the reckless endangerment and unlawful imprisonment charges. We told both men we would allow them to sign their own bond on the hunter harassment charge.

We lined up both men to meet us at the county jail on a Saturday afternoon. We were standing outside our vehicles when Mr. Erikson arrived. He was early. Mr. Erikson, who was six feet seven inches tall, got out of his vehicle and approached us. The first thing he said was he had brought his son with him in case we decided to put him in jail. We advised him we did not plan to do that and he responded that we might after we heard what he had to say. I'll admit that piqued our interest. We moved inside to a deputy office.

CEO Hayes told Mr. Erikson we needed to advise him of his rights. He gave him a Miranda rights form and he read and signed it. He advised us he had spoken with an attorney who had told him not to make a statement. We told him that was fine. Having been through this procedure hundreds of times, I felt things were over with. Therefore, I'm sure there was an interesting look on my face when he, unprompted, said, "This is what happened." He began telling an interesting story. He said he was just there to help his friend (Mr. Dye) who was a really good guy. He stated he was there to "back him up" because the hunter was hunting too close to the property line with his gun pointed toward Mr. Dye's property. He said he and Mr. Dye were out on the property a lot as were Mr. Dye's children. He said their intention was just to keep things safe.

Drake advised him of the charge he was charged with and he stated he did not think that was right. He said he had been hunting several times when he had someone come up on him and he had never got upset about it. He said someone coming up on you doesn't mess up your hunt and many times after someone comes up a deer may come through shortly after that.

Without any prompting he continued to discuss the situation. He said he did not think the hunter should have been upset seeing how he had a rifle. At this point, I asked Mr. Erikson if he had a rifle and he replied he did not. I knew this was in contrast to what Mr. Dye had told Deputy Rudd on video and what he had told us as well. It is very common for suspects to downplay their role in the activity they are being questioned about.

We advised him of the court date and time. He said he would have to take a day off of work and we were costing him a lot of money. He again stated his attorney had told him not to say any more than a broad statement. I could not help but think that all he had just told us was not at all what the attorney had intended! He reiterated everything about the encounter with the hunter was friendly and they had shaken hands and exchanged phone numbers. He said he was there to protect his buddy because there had been some suspicious activity in the past including someone driving up the driveway that morning. He repeated he didn't think he should be charged with anything and he left.

Once he was out the door I looked at Drake and said I was glad he didn't want to give a statement because if he had we would have been there all day! When we emerged from the office, Mr. Dye was in the sheriff's office lobby. He had arranged for a local bail bondsman to meet him there. We provided them with the necessary paperwork and left.

Prior to the court date we received word the pair had obtained legal counsel and a continuance had been requested and granted. Therefore, it would be another month before the cases came to court.

The next month we were in court and ready. At this point we learned the pair had hired a high-powered attorney from the nearby town of Sylacauga to represent them. This was some consolation for us in that in the event we were to lose the case, we knew they were already out about $5,000. The attorney asked the ADA if he could speak with him. They went into the ADA office and discussed the case.

According to the ADA, once he had laid out our case, the attorney asked what it would take to settle things. Based on our strong case, we had anticipated this and had a plea agreement in mind. It was decided Mr. Dye would plead guilty to false imprisonment and hunter harassment. On the false imprisonment charge he received a twelve-month suspended sentence. He was placed on two years of unsupervised probation. He was given a no contact order and trespassed from the hunting club property. He was assessed fines and court costs of $978. On the hunter harassment charge he was given a ten-day suspended sentence and fined $500. Mr. Erikson received a ten-day suspended sentence and a $500 fine on the hunter harassment charge. The fines and court costs combined with the attorney fee brought the total to around $7,000!

As I mentioned earlier, this case had the potential to go sideways very quickly. Confronting someone with a loaded gun in their hand is a dangerous proposition. Believe me, I know. This is compounded greatly when the person who instigates the confrontation has no authority to do so. As was stated by some of the folks involved, if someone else had been the person confronted, this could have had a deadly conclusion.

Had the hunter actually been only twenty yards across the property line, he would have still been legal. However, the adjacent landowner's concern would have been more understandable.

Every year we receive calls from folks complaining about people hunting the property line and looking onto their property. The reports are often legitimate, although they aren't easy to act on. However, in most cases the people complained about are not thirteen times farther away than the landowner claims! Credibility is a major factor in each trial. Not only did the defendant in this case lack credibility, he was also a really poor judge of distance!

Can You Take a Hint?
(Evidently Not)

THE DISTRICT JUDGE WAS DOING HIS BEST to assist the defendant; however, it appeared the violator was having none of it. At first, it was if it the fellow could not understand the inflection in the judge's voice. Soon it was apparent the fellow didn't understand much of anything.

District court judges could be a source of angst or a source of joy and sometimes both. They were the first stop for our cases in the judicial system and 98 percent of the time things were handled there and did not go any further. I have written many times how much I appreciated district judges who carried the sword for mother nature. Unfortunately, not all judges held a soft spot for conservation. The judge's physical and mental proximity to the outdoors was important. I could understand how a judge who had little exposure to nature would think some of our fines were outrageous. The judge who had experienced someone shooting in his yard at night often felt our fines were entirely appropriate!

Late in my career, due to pressure from legislatures and other groups, judges often found their hands tied when it came to passing out sentences. Judges that wanted to hammer violators were restricted in what they could do and those who wanted to be excessively lenient were empowered to do so.

I had the opportunity to bring several cases before judges in surrounding counties and quickly learned each one was somewhat unique in how they handled the courtroom. What was most common, especially for conservation violations, was for the defendants to stand before the bench and offer their plea. If they pled guilty the judge normally immediately sentenced them. Sometimes the officer involved was given the opportunity to provide pertinent information and sometimes the judge proceeded without any further input. In the event the person pled not guilty, the officer would be called on to testify. Some courts, none that I appeared in, advised the officers they were not needed for court. In these situations, defendants who pled guilty were sentenced by the judge and if someone desired a trial the officer would be contacted and advised of the trial date. The fact that many of these scenarios resulted in the violators handling their own case resulted in many interesting conversations at the judge's bench.

As certified police officers in the state of Alabama, it wasn't totally unusual for us to perform enforcement activities outside our normal scope. This might mean we were called on to assist a county deputy at a domestic dispute, assist a state trooper at an accident, or stop an erratic driver and take them to jail for driving under the influence. Obviously, this wasn't our desired activity; however, we took things as they came. One area where we regularly crossed paths with another enforcement agency was on the water.

When I began my career, the Alabama Marine Police were a brother agency in the department of conservation. It was not at all unusual for a marine police officer to check someone's fishing license and it wasn't unusual for us to check a boater's registration and safety equipment. Late in my career, the marine police were pulled from our department and placed under the Alabama Law Enforcement Agency, making them state troopers. While this changed some things, we continued to check boat safety equipment.

No matter what activity you are talking about, you've probably heard someone say safety should be the first priority. That is definitely true when you are talking about hunting and boating. One of the worst parts of my job was having to work a hunting accident. I feel certain it was the same for the marine police who were tasked with working boating accidents. There are several laws and regulations in place to try to keep these activities safe. As I mentioned earlier, we regularly would check a boater's safety equipment when checking fishing on lakes and rivers.

Conservation Enforcement Officer Ryan O'Meara was assigned to Tallapoosa County which carried with it the responsibility of patrolling Lake Martin. The man-made lake was 44,000 acres in size and had 750 miles of shoreline. If you are thinking there was probably a lot of boating on the lake, you would be correct. On Labor Day the normal number of boaters on the water reported by the media was thirty thousand! When you have that many folks on the water, you definitely hope they are abiding by the safety rules. Of course, the safety rules are important even if yours is the only boat on the lake.

Required safety equipment varied by the size and type of boat. For most fishing boats the primary requirement was personal flotation devices for everyone on board. Beyond that and depending on the size of the boat folks were required to have a throwable flotation device, a horn or sounding device, an attachable kill switch, and a functioning fire extinguisher. I hope the need for a fire extinguisher on a boat with a motor is evident. However, I have met several boaters who did not find it necessary to possess one. I always found it interesting when a boater without an extinguisher would say they were surrounded by water and they could always just jump in. Yes, I got that response more than once.

As you can imagine, a fire extinguisher that stays in a boat exposed to the elements year-round would quickly deteriorate. This was especially true with the cheapest disposable model which seemed to be the favorite of many fishermen. This was often a problem in that these units did not hold a charge for a long time. The regulation states the unit must be functional. This was the bane of many a boater.

CEO O'Meara had checked a young fisherman on the lake and found that his extinguisher was not functional. After explaining to the man the necessity of having a working extinguisher, he wrote the man a ticket. This type of citation was referred to by some officers and judges as a "fix it" ticket. That meant if the violation had been corrected before the individual appeared in court, the charge would likely be dropped.

A month later, the defendant stood before the judge. The judge advised he had been charged with failing to have a serviceable fire extinguisher. The defendant appeared to be in his early twenties. I would quickly learn he wasn't the most perceptive individual in the courtroom. The judge asked, "Have you bought a fire extinguisher?" The defendant responded, "No." He then added, "My boss gave me one." The judge, sensing an opportunity to help the young man out, said, "So you have one in your boat now?" The man replied, "No, I put it in my truck." The judge hopefully and suggestively said, "But you will put it in your boat?" and the defendant replied, "No, it's too hot to fish." It was evident someone must have told him that no matter what the question was he should answer with a "no."

Realizing he was not getting through to the man, the judge just shook his head and said, "Okay, the fine is fifty dollars and the cost is more than that so I'm just going to charge you fifty dollars total." The judge asked, "Have you got fifty dollars?" The guy stuck to the script and said, "No." He then added, "I have sixty dollars." The judge rolled his eyes and told the fellow to go pay the clerk. Some folks just can't take a hint!

You can't make this stuff up.

Just Trying to Catch a Deer

A POPULAR QUOTE READS, "The only thing necessary for the triumph of evil is for good men to do nothing." I feel fairly certain that Edmund Burke probably wasn't referring to people not reporting illegal hunting activity; however, the principle is the same. All it takes for violators to damage our wildlife resources is for the folks who know it's occurring to say nothing. Fortunately, some folks realize these wildlife outlaws are stealing from them and stand up and give a voice to wildlife.

The early December morning was progressing like most others. Sixteen-year-old Holly Conner was headed to high school. While living on Lake Martin was great, the twisting, turning narrow roads near the lake were not that fun to navigate. As she drove along narrow Beach Crest Drive and prepared to turn onto Ivy Green Road she observed a white SUV sitting in the road near the intersection. There she observed a man who was later identified as Olin Sprott. She described Mr. Sprott as having a bow and arrow in his hand and stated he was crouched down and walking as if stalking a deer. She said when he saw her, he turned and walked behind the white SUV. She noted there was a man wearing an orange shirt sitting in the driver's seat.

After turning onto Ivy Green Road and passing the SUV, looking in her rearview mirror she observed that Mr. Sprott was once again stalking across the road. Knowing deer regularly frequented the lot where the man was, Ms. Conner phoned her mother and reported what she had witnessed. Mrs. Conner was also driving along Beach Crest Drive and soon met the vehicle matching the description her daughter had provided. She in turn phoned her husband and relayed what her daughter had told her and the description and direction of travel of the vehicle.

Mr. Conner phoned Conservation Enforcement Officer (CEO) Ryan O'Meara and advised him of what had occurred. Mr. Conner drove through the neighborhood looking for the suspect vehicle and eventually located it at a construction site. It seemed there was always construction taking place around the lake, which generated a good deal of traffic. Mr. Conner took a photo of the vehicle's license plate and sent it to Officer O'Meara. CEO O'Meara ran the tag and found the vehicle was registered to Mr. Olin Sprott. The address was in neighboring Lee County.

Just because a tag number comes back to someone, it doesn't mean that is your violator. In this case, the primary violator appeared to be the passenger in the vehicle. One would assume the one driving the vehicle would be the owner and the registration would come back to the owner. You may have heard a little saying about assuming something! While we were not sure the vehicle owner was our suspect, we did at least have a starting point. If Mr. Sprott was indeed the driver, he should know the identity of the person out on the ground. I hope you noticed I said *should*. You would likely be surprised to learn how often folks hang around with folks they don't know. I mean they don't even know their names! Many times, I have checked a couple of people standing a short distance apart and fishing. Once I have checked the first one I sometimes ask them what their buddy's name is. They often reply they don't know the other person. Interestingly enough, I move to the other person and check their license and ask if they know the other guy and they say, "Yeah, he's my brother." I kid you not. This happens much more often than one would think. I was questioning a woman one day about the actions of her grandson. When I asked his name, she stated she did not know it. I said, "You don't know your own sixteen-year-old grandson's name?" "No" was her answer. I told her I found that hard to believe and she said, "We call him Pookie." I digress. I do that a lot.

This was CEO O'Meara's first full hunting season after completing the police academy so he was still wet behind the ears but was a quick study. He knew just having a tag number was a long way from having a viable suspect. Therefore, he worked with the sheriff's office to develop a photo array which included a photo of our suspect and five other similar looking individuals.

He traveled to the Conner home and took a statement from Ms. Holly Conner. He showed her the photo array and she immediately identified Mr. Sprott as the man she had observed with the bow. Things were definitely beginning to look up. It seemed the owner of the vehicle was actually the one out "stalking" across the road.

O'Meara gave me a call and told me what had occurred. As he told me the story, I asked if the sixteen-year-old girl actually said she thought the man was "stalking" a deer. He said that was what she had said and she had clarified the statement by saying she was a bowhunter and knew what it looked like for someone to stalk a deer. I told him that was some great detail to have in a statement. I advised him I felt we needed to go and take a look at the scene.

The next day I met Ryan and we traveled to the area where the incident had taken place. We stopped at the intersection where the witness had said she observed the white SUV and subject in the road with his bow. I noted there were two houses close by and told Ryan we needed to talk with those residents and take some measurements. We went on to the Conner's house and found Mr. Conner working in his shop. He explained after his wife had called, he had driven around the neighborhood until he spotted a white SUV matching the description he had been given. He had not spoken to anyone at the scene but had taken a photo of the license plate which he had forwarded to CEO O'Meara. We asked if he knew which construction company was doing the work where he saw the vehicle and he said he thought it was Worldwide Construction. Ryan took a statement from Mr. Conner. He told him with his daughter's help we had identified the suspect and our intention was to obtain warrants for him. We explained that while we would try to avoid a trial, it was possible his daughter would need to testify. We asked if he thought he would want to allow her to do that. He did not hesitate and said he definitely wanted her to testify if needed. He went on to say he had been teaching her to hunt and had stressed to her it was important to follow the rules and he thought this would be a good way to stress that point. While I definitely wanted the young girl to testify if needed, I felt it was imperative we let Mr. Conner know our suspect was a convicted felon. It was not for a crime of violence; however, he was a felon nonetheless. He stated he would be able to protect his daughter. We thanked him and told him we would be in touch.

Back in our vehicle, I told Ryan it might be a good idea to see if we could find the vehicle at one of the many construction sites in the area and if so talk with our suspect. I have found that many times when you catch a suspect off guard it turns out better than when you call them in for an "official" interview. We checked numerous construction areas but did not see a vehicle matching the description.

We returned to the intersection of Beach Crest and Ivy Green and pulled off the side of the road. We reviewed Holly's statement and got a good feel of where things were on the day of the incident. Directly across the road where she said the fellow had stalked across was a small grassy opening with a utility shed on one side. Examination of the area revealed several piles of deer droppings. This aligned well with Holly saying she had frequently seen deer in the area.

There were also two houses in the area. Examination of the property revealed the hunting had taken place within ninety-three yards of one residence and sixty-five yards from another. Alabama law says it is illegal to hunt within one hundred yards of a dwelling. Therefore, we felt Mr. Sprott was definitely in violation of that law.

We went to the nearest residence but there was no one home. We went to the other residence and there met Mr. Elias Shinbone. We introduced ourselves and explained to him we were investigating a road hunting incident that had occurred on his property. He was visibly shaken when he realized someone was attempting to shoot a deer so close to his home. He stated there were two families of deer that lived on his property and he did not allow any hunting whatsoever! He went on to say he hoped the judge would put who did this in jail. We told him we were going to do our best to see that justice was served.

The next week I met with CEO O'Meara and our other partner, CEO Jinks Altiere, and we discussed the situation. We decided based on our evidence, we would go ahead and obtain warrants on Mr. Sprott for hunting from a public road, hunting without a permit, hunting too close to a dwelling, and hunting without wearing any hunter orange. Although bowhunters aren't required to wear hunter orange during archery-only season, they are required to wear it while on the ground during gun deer season. We also discussed whether or not to pursue any charges against the driver of the vehicle. Of course, at this time, we did not know who that was or what role they may have played in the incident. Therefore, we decided we would wait and see what our suspect would tell us.

During the course of the investigation we learned Mr. Sprott was on probation in Lee County. This made things somewhat easier in that people on probation are required to check in regularly with their probation officer (PO) and are to comply with whatever their PO tells them to do. Ryan contacted the PO and asked him to have Mr. Sprott meet us at the Tallapoosa County jail.

On the appointed day, the suspect arrived at the jail and CEO's O'Meara, Altiere, and I escorted him back to an investigator's office which would serve as our interrogation room. We advised him of his rights and he signed a waiver. CEO O'Meara asked if he knew what incident we were there to discuss. This is a good question since, believe it or not, we have had folks begin telling us about an incident we knew nothing about until they shared it with us! Mr. Sprott stated he understood someone had said they had seen him hunting. He went on to say he was on Ivy Green Road early that morning but he was not hunting. He was on his way to a construction site where he and his son were working. He said later that morning someone came and took pictures of his vehicle at the construction site. I asked if it was his son who was driving the vehicle that morning and he said it was and he himself rarely drove the vehicle. I asked if he remembered whether or not his son was wearing an orange shirt and he said he did not. I asked if he carried his bow with him to work and he said sometimes he did in case he was able to get off early and go hunting. He went on to say he was addicted to hunting.

While all this information generally lined up with what we knew, I knew we needed more. I asked the man why the witness would have said they saw him out of the vehicle and stalking a deer. This was when it got interesting. He initially answered that he wasn't out of the vehicle. It was then that I employed two tried-and-true tactics. First, I didn't say anything. As I like to phrase it, I just let it hang in the air. I have found that silence will tear down some people's defenses. Second, I gave him "the look." As I have taught many officers, you must develop your "You're lying and it disgusts me" look. While some folks can't handle silence, others can't handle the look. Believe me, I've used both of these techniques hundreds of times. Mr. Sprott was no different. After we sat in silence and I gave him the look, he said, "I might be telling on myself, but I might have been out of the vehicle trying to catch a deer!" I immediately responded, "Trying to catch a deer?" He said his boss had told him if you saw a young deer sometimes you could run at it and it would squat down and you could catch it. I asked, "Have you ever caught one?" He said, "No." And I said, "But that was what you were trying to do?" and he said, "It could have been, that area is full of deer." While I felt he was thinking he had come up with a viable defense, I was thinking he had just put himself out of the vehicle and attempting to catch a deer. I asked if he had been wearing any hunter orange on that day and he said he had not. I asked if he had any per-mission to hunt anywhere in the area and he said he did not.

We stepped out of the room and conferred for a minute. I asked Ryan and Jinks if they could think of anything else to ask and they both agreed we had probably gotten all we were going to. However, I did have one more question I wanted to ask him.

We returned to the room and I asked Mr. Sprott what had resulted in his felony theft case. He did not hesitate and said he had been arrested for collecting road signs. I must admit that wasn't what I had expected to hear. I thought to myself, how many or which road signs did you have to steal for it to constitute a felony arrest. He volunteered he had signs covering the walls of his barn and he had been collecting them all of his life. He clarified that to say he had only taken signs that had been knocked down or run over or something. Yeah, right.

Ryan informed the man we had warrants for his arrest and advised him of the charges. He told him since he was on probation, his PO would need to know about these charges and he could have him put in jail for violating his probation but that we were going to allow him to sign his bonds. He signed the bonds and was advised of the court date.

The court date came around and the defendant and his wife were in the courtroom. Unfortunately, our witnesses were not. It turned out our witnesses were on a family vacation and did not appear despite having been subpoenaed. Obviously, that was a problem. We met with the ADA and decided if the defendant wanted to plead guilty we would drop two of the charges which would save him approximately fifteen hundred dollars. We decided to make the offer seeing how the judge could easily dismiss the case since our witnesses were not present. The ADA approached the man with the offer and was told he wasn't pleading to anything. The ADA came back and informed the judge we would like to have the case continued until the next month. The judge agreed to continue the case; however, he said in no uncertain terms the case would be heard the next month.

I believe the judge meant what he said; however, he had no way of knowing that a little something called COVID-19 was going to come along. The COVID-19 virus wreaked havoc on the court system, like it did on so many other things. Court was suspended for months and came back piece by piece. Finally, late in the summer, several months after the incident, the case was once again set for trial.

Unfortunately, by this time CEO O'Meara's National Guard unit had been deployed to assist with the COVID-19 crisis. Of course, this threw a wrench in things in that he would have to get permission to come back and attend the trial. With a new trial date set, Ryan began the process of getting permission to attend the proceedings. Seeing how Ryan had been the one to sign the warrants, it was imperative that he be in court. Arrangements were made and we were all set. We had reviewed our notes and felt that we were as ready as we could be. Little did I know something that had never happened in my career was about to happen.

At 9:50 p.m. the night before our trial was scheduled at 9:00 a.m. the next morning, I received a text message from the ADA saying the judge had granted the defendant a continuance and the trial would have to be rescheduled. My first thought was had he just now got around to continuing the case! Obviously having had court cases for thirty-plus years, I have had several cases continued. Just like the first time this came to court, I have had cases continued while standing before the judge. However, I had never been notified at ten o'clock at night that a case set for the next morning had been continued. Of course, with COVID, there were a lot of firsts happening. While this continuance was aggravating for me, it was really aggravating for Ryan after he had to get permission to be there. Things happen.

I kept in touch with the ADA and finally a new court date was set. It was forty-five days short of being one year since the event had occurred. The ADA assured me the case would be heard on that date. Since the last court date, Ryan had been redeployed meaning he would once again have to gain permission to attend the trial. We again reviewed our notes and prepared for the trial.

In going over my notes, I realized something I hadn't really thought about previously. As I told you earlier, in an effort to say he wasn't hunting a deer, he had said he may have been trying to catch a deer. When I got to thinking about his statement, I realized when you think about the definition of hunting that is printed in our regulation book, the defendant basically confessed to the charges we were charging him with. The definition of hunting printed in the Alabama regulation book states hunting includes pursuing, shooting, killing, capturing, and trapping wild animals, wild fowl, wild birds, and all lesser acts, such as disturbing, harrying or worrying, or placing, setting, drawing, or using any device used to take wild animals, wild fowl, wild birds, whether they result in taking or not, and includes every act of assistance to any person in taking or attempting to take wild animals, wild fowl, or wild birds.

Finally, the appointed date was upon us. I texted Ryan and reminded him of the date and asked that he once again get the okay to attend. He sarcastically wrote back he would believe it when he saw it. I was sort of having the same feeling. I was really ready to get this case over with. With the court date set for Thursday, I contacted the ADA on Monday. He assured me the witnesses were lined up and everything was set. Of course, you know we don't control everything! The fact that 2020 was a year like no other in many ways was about to be proven again.

In addition to being struck with a worldwide pandemic, 2020 was also plagued with massive wildfires and hurricanes. There were so many hurricanes that the weather service blew through the slate of selected names and then had to go to a rarely used system where they used the letters of the Greek alphabet to name storms. The hurricanes just kept coming and we were now at the Greek name Zeta. Early in the week the meteorologists were predicting that Zeta was going to have a significant impact on Alabama. While hurricanes impacting the gulf coast is certainly nothing new, when they cause widespread damage two hundred miles inland, that is definitely deviant from the norm.

So, with the trial pending the next morning I went to bed wondering how this was going to play out. Actually, I did not go to bed. I sat up with my wife and we watched as the storm made landfall and seemed to head straight for us. My wife had packed a bag and was ready to head to the basement. After we watched the weather at 10 p.m., she went to the basement. I continued to watch television until the storm got bad enough that it knocked out the signal. I then joined her in the basement and we listened to my sheriff's office radio.

The winds reached speeds of sixty-two miles an hour. When you combined that with a few inches of rain to loosen the soil, it wasn't long until trees were hitting the ground all over the place. We rode out the worst of the storm in the basement. It wasn't long until the sheriff's office dispatchers were getting pretty frazzled with hundreds of calls coming in. I had anticipated this and already had my uniform on. At 2:30 a.m. the deputies on duty were calling for assistance so I headed out to assist as I could.

I called our dispatcher on the radio but received no answer. I called the radio room on the phone but only got static. I decided our communications must have been a casualty of the storm. As I pulled out of my driveway, I went west toward the county seat of Rockford. I picked up the sheriff's office radio microphone and called dispatch. I told the dispatcher I had intended to tell her I was in service; however, seeing how I was now looking at a huge red oak tree that covered both lanes of Highway 22, I told her she needed to add another tree to her growing list. I backed away from the tree until I reached an area where I could turn around and headed east on the highway. I traveled about one-half mile before I came upon a large pine tree blocking both lanes. Just about twenty yards past it was another, bigger tree occupying both lanes. I contemplated trying to maneuver around the tree but the several inches of rain associated with the storm made the ditch full of standing water more than I dared to tackle.

Eventually I saw headlights approaching. My first impression was one of the several volunteer fire departments that were now trying to remove trees was working their way toward me. I was mistaken. A fellow in a car hauler with a roll back bed pulled up to where I sat with my blue lights flashing. He exited his truck and came over to me and said if he could get around the end of the first tree he could use the winch on the rear of his rig to move the other tree out of the road. I had not anticipated him saying that and I didn't really say anything. I guess he either thought my silence was permission to try it or he was going to do what he wanted to. I think it was the latter.

He got in his truck and drove through the top of the pine that was blocking the road. Once on the other side, he maneuvered his truck so that he could use the winch on the back to pull the large pine tree far enough to open one lane of the road. I trailed along behind him as he repeated the procedure six or seven times.

As I was following him down the road, I came upon a fellow in a jacked up four-wheel-drive pickup. I asked where he was headed and he said, "Rockford." I told him he could make it but one lane was blocked in several places and he needed to proceed with caution. He said OK and then pulled out and went in the opposite direction from Rockford. I followed him as he followed the guy in the tow truck who was clearing out the roads. We traveled this way for two or three miles. I had stopped to cut back some limbs when I saw the truck had turned around and was now heading back toward me. I stopped him and said, "I thought you were going to Rockford." He replied he didn't know what had happened but he had sure gotten turned around.

I continued to check roads and report blockages to the sheriff's office. Most every road in the county was blocked to some extent. There were numerous traffic accidents, some severe, where drivers had failed to slow down and had run into trees in the road. Numerous houses were damaged as well. Once again, we were blessed in that there was no loss of life.

I felt certain our long-delayed court case would once again be continued. I was wrong. I contacted CEO O'Meara and he agreed there likely would not be any court. My calls to the district attorney's office were not answered. I decided to send a text to the ADA just to be sure. I was shocked when he replied court was still a go. I had now been awake for almost twenty-eight hours and I was definitely dragging. I texted the ADA and let him know I would be en route; however, I would be having to dodge several trees in the road and would likely be late. I cleaned up as best I could, donned my class A uniform, and headed for Tallapoosa County.

I had contacted CEO O'Meara and told him I would be by shortly to pick him up. I contacted our other partner, CEO Altiere, and learned the roads in his neighborhood were totally blocked with trees and he would not be able to make it to court.

Ryan and I arrived at the courthouse at about 9:20 a.m. We put on our masks and entered the building. Due to COVID-19, courthouse security checked our temperature. We headed upstairs to the courtroom and met the ADA in the hallway. He said the defendant was present. He also told us our witness was in the grand jury room and we might want to go and meet with her and her dad. He said he would like for one of us to provide the facts of the case to the judge and he would ask any necessary questions.

Ryan told me he thought it would be best if I would handle giving the testimony and I told him I would be glad to fill in any details he might miss, but that he would be giving the initial testimony. I think he knew that was coming; however, the look on his face said he wasn't sure he was ready for that. It would be the first time he had had to give any extended testimony and that can be somewhat intimidating. I told him we would rehearse it. Unfortunately, most rooms had people in them; therefore, we found a spot in the hallway where we could run through the testimony. I told Ryan to start with when he received the call about the incident and go from there. As he worked through what all had occurred, I made sure he included all the elements of the charges. After a couple of times through it, he seemed to have it down pretty well.

We went down the hall to the grand jury room and found our sixteen-year-old witness and her father there. The young lady was very composed and did not seem nervous at all. We discussed how things would likely go in the courtroom. I told her all she needed to do was tell the story the same way she had told it initially and answer any questions from the ADA or judge.

Unfortunately, trials normally are held after all other cases are worked out. Today was no different. Finally, the ADA stuck his head in the door and told us they were ready for us. Our witness and her dad moved to the jury room next to the courtroom and Ryan and I entered the courtroom. The ADA stepped up to the bench and told the judge we were ready to proceed. The judge called the defendant up and informed him that since the charges carried possible jail time, he was appointing him an attorney. This was the first time this judge had appointed an attorney in any case I had ever brought before his court. Ryan looked at me and with his eyes asked how this was going to change things. I told him this didn't change a thing. I assured him we had a rock-solid case and there was nothing to worry about. I thought to myself I hoped the attorney didn't batter him with a lot of questions because that's not something you want to have happen when it's your first time testifying. However, this lawyer had represented some folks I had arrested previously and had been easy to work with in those cases.

The attorney met briefly with his client and then approached us. He said the defendant would plead guilty to hunting without a permit and hunting too close to a dwelling if we would drop the other two charges. I told him we would consider that but we needed to confer with our witness. The attorney said, "You can tell them they've done their job seeing how he's willing to confess." I thought that was an interesting comment. We approached the ADA and told him what they had offered. From the beginning we had hoped our young witness would not have to testify and this way she would not even be identified. Looking at it from that standpoint, we felt it was a win-win situation. The ADA agreed. We stepped into the jury room and explained to our witness and her dad what we were considering. The said it was fine with them and the decision was made.

We returned to the courtroom and informed the counselor we would accept that deal. He informed his client and the guy immediately jumped up and yelled, "Thank you!" The lawyer again approached us and said his client was scared to death he was going to lose his hunting privileges. I told him the permit case did allow the judge to take his privileges for a year. I looked at Ryan and asked what he thought. He said he didn't care. I told the attorney that we would not request that the judge revoke his privileges. He went back and informed his client, who again yelled out, "Thank you!" He then said, "I will never break the law again," followed by, "I'm even going to start measuring my fish!" I must admit I had never had anyone say that before. In our area, while not the only one, the primary fish that had to be measured was crappie, which could not be kept if they weren't at least nine inches long. Of course, his statement told me that was another law he had been violating in the past.

The judge motioned for everyone to approach the bench and asked if we had reached an agreement. The defense attorney told him we had and the defendant would be pleading on two cases. The judge said, "On hunting without a permit, how do you plead?" The man answered, "Guilty." The judge looked at me and asked what was the fine and I told him it was $1,000. He asked the man how he pled on the charge of hunting too close to a dwelling and he again answered, "Guilty." The judge again looked at me and I told him the fine was $100. The judge said the other two charges would be dismissed. The defendant said, "I want to thank all of y'all. I was an addict and I've been clean for six years. Hunting allowed me to get clean and stay clean and I appreciate you not taking that away from me and I will never break the law again." It had been a long time since I had heard anything so heartfelt in the courtroom.

We returned to the jury room. We told our witness and her dad how it had gone. They were happy she wouldn't have to testify and were satisfied with the outcome. We thanked them and I told her incidents of illegal hunting, like the one she had observed, happen every day. The difference is most people choose not to get involved. I told her we appreciated her willingness to report the incident and to testify if necessary. I told her a lot of adults could learn from her example.

This was a great teaching case. It had a lot of ins and outs and required a good bit of preparation. Afterward I explained to Ryan it's much better to be well prepared and not have to testify than to be unprepared and have a defense attorney make you look like an idiot. Ryan had the makings of a good conservation officer; however, he decided to accept a full-time position with the national guard. Our loss was their good fortune. I may be wrong but I doubt he will soon forget the guy who was just trying to catch a deer!

Extreme
Aiding and Abetting

A LOT OF GAME AND FISH OUTLAWS avoid apprehension by being assisted by family, friends, and even strangers. This assistance is normally in the form of keeping quiet about the violator's activities. That is often true with family and friends and surprisingly also with strangers. Many times, I have had a landowner contact me about someone hunting illegally on their property. They give what details they have and advise they would like to have the activity stopped. Unfortunately, after that they often add they don't want to get anybody in trouble.

At this point I normally make them aware of a couple of things. Number one, if you don't want the person who is illegally hunting on your property arrested, then I'm not your person. I have seen several hunting-without-a-permit cases where it literally took years to catch the culprit. I don't want to spend that kind of time on a case only to have a landowner say they don't want to charge the violator. Number two, I tell landowners that when poachers understand they will not be prosecuted, they might as well give them a permit to hunt the property. In addition, someone hunting on your property without permission is dangerous. I realize I'm biased, but having spent thirty-seven years chasing wildlife outlaws, I feel they need to be apprehended. Of course, the aiding and abetting of outlaws wasn't limited to us!

District court is an interesting place. I think everyone should attend a session of court. It can really be an eye-opening experience. The first time I was ever in court was as an arresting officer. I learned a few things rather quickly. One thing I picked up was to never take anything for granted.

Surprises in the courtroom were common. It was interesting when folks who were the most apologetic and humble in the field would come to court and enthusiastically plead not guilty and lie about everything that had happened. Others who in the field cussed you like a dog and left saying "I'll see you in court" would end up pleading guilty and paying off prior to the court date.

While I often felt we had dealt with almost everything imaginable, I was routinely reminded that wasn't the case. The things people will do are amazing. In our district court all of the misdemeanor cases from all agencies were heard on the same day. That meant there would normally be state troopers, game wardens, sheriff's deputies, corrections officers, and officers from the two municipalities in the county in the courtroom. This set the stage for some interesting happenings.

I was in court one Wednesday morning and things were going along as usual when I noticed the jail administrator come through the door and make a bee line to the chief deputy. He whispered something in his ear and the chief immediately summoned a couple of deputies and they all left the courtroom. I had no idea what might be going on and there was really no way to know. While I could have followed them outside, I was interested in the case before the judge and one of my cases was next on the docket so I didn't need to leave. Shortly, the jail administrator came over to me and whispered in my ear a phrase I often use. He said, "You can't make this stuff up." Of course, that piqued my interest.

We moved off to the side of the courtroom and he asked if I was familiar with the case where the woman was under suspicion for aiding and abetting an escape from the work release center in the county. I told him I had heard something about it. He told me she was on the docket today and was seated at the end of the front row. So far this wasn't anything too unusual but it was about to be.

He said one of the jailers had walked past her car in the parking lot and saw the escapee sitting in the front seat. The jailer told him and he advised the chief deputy. The deputies went down and took the man into custody. He said the investigators were preparing a warrant for her arrest and planned to arrest her when the judge called her case.

Shortly thereafter the judge called for a brief recess. In an unusual move he asked everyone to remain in the courtroom and he would be back momentarily. I realized this was giving the court the time to secure the warrant and was keeping the woman from leaving the courtroom to go and check on her boyfriend.

In a couple of minutes, the judge returned to the bench and resumed court. He called the female defendant to the bench and advised her that a warrant had been sworn for her arrest and the deputies moved in and took her into custody.

In my opinion, that's a pretty good example of things you just can't make up! The next time you have a free day, go and attend district court. You might just see or hear something you won't believe.

A Night Hunter
Like No Other

I HAVE WRITTEN MANY STORIES about night hunting. It would be interesting to know how many nights I have spent working trying to catch folks hunting after dark. Having worked for thirty-seven years, it would be a lot of nights. I have witnessed a lot of things and been surprised on several occasions. Having worked as long as I have, I know better than to think I've seen it all. I've seen a lot of things I'm sure people probably don't believe; however, none of it had prepared me for what I witnessed one cold January night near Lake Martin in Tallapoosa County.

After I retired I did what I think most folks do. I had a long list of projects I had let slide and I set about working on them. I made good progress and whittled the list down fairly quickly. Within a few months an offer of part-time employment as a conservation enforcement officer was tendered and I jumped at the chance. Due to promotions and transfers, there were no officers in Tallapoosa County. Seeing how I lived adjacent to the county and was fairly familiar with it, I was rehired. I began on October 1.

Tallapoosa County is a great hunting and fishing county. There are plenty of deer and turkey and abundant small game. The county is rural enough that there is ample hunting opportunity. The county is a water enthusiast's paradise. In addition to the Tallapoosa River, the county is home to the largest man-made lake in the country, Lake Martin. The lake is forty-four thousand acres in size providing ample room for both angling and boating. Of course, if you've ever done either one of these activities, you know they don't normally get along too well together. Unfortunately, I never had done a lot of work out of a boat and those skills definitely needed some honing.

The deer season had not been overly active. We had made the occasional baiting case and answered various hunting-without-a-permit calls. The land around the lake is sliced up in every kind of shape you can imagine. When you factor in that much of the lake property is bordered by industrial forest land, which is leased for hunting, you can see where there would be conflicts. However, they were not all that common. However, like in any county in Alabama where deer are known to frequent, which is all of them, there was night hunting.

It did not take long to locate a good spot to work night hunting. A simple nighttime ride down Alabama Highway 63 South revealed numerous night hunting targets. On a good night it wasn't unusual to see forty deer in about a four-mile stretch of the road. Unfortunately, there aren't many residences along the road; therefore, we did not receive many complaints. However, I have worked long enough to know that having a high number of deer standing along the side of the road in an area with few houses was more temptation than a lot of folks could stand. Needless to say, we spent a pretty good amount of time in the area.

In late January it had already been a long season. The long days and nights begin to take their toll after you've been working deer hunting for three months. Seeing how the gun deer season had been extended until February 10, we still had another month to go. However, catching a night hunter provided a rush that I needed so I dutifully set up in my hiding spot near Russell Farms Church and started my vigil.

I was not alone in this endeavor. CEO Johnny Johnson Jr. had transferred to our department from the Department of Corrections where he had been a dog handler. This was his first deer season and he was still learning the ropes. He was set up approximately two miles south of me on the same highway. It was always good to have someone close by when working at night in our rural landscape.

We had been in place for almost two hours when at approximately 11:45 p.m. I heard what sounded like a small-caliber rifle shot. I estimated the shot was less than one-half mile south of my location. There had not been any vehicles traveling south in the past few minutes so I surmised the vehicle was coming north. I radioed CEO Johnson and told him to come toward me. Within a few seconds I saw headlights coming from the south. I allowed the vehicle to pass my location and I pulled out behind it. As I came over a small rise, I observed the vehicle stopped in the road. I activated my blue lights and pulled up behind the vehicle.

I called the Tallapoosa County Sheriff's Office dispatcher and gave them the tag number of the Ford Crown Victoria car. As I approached the vehicle, I observed three occupants. A driver, a front seat passenger, and a rear seat passenger on the driver's side. I also observed a rifle that was against the rear passenger side door. I immediately thought that was an odd place for the gun to be; however, I was also thinking that might not be the only gun.

As you can imagine, approaching a vehicle from which someone has just shot in the middle of the night is a little nerve wracking. I gave the loud verbal command for the occupants to put their hands up. The passengers immediately complied but the driver did not. Moving to where I could see the driver better, I ordered him to put his hands on the steering wheel. I noticed there was movement but his hands did not come up. Several things were going through my mind. In my experience, when you order someone to raise their hands and they fail to do so there is a reason for their noncompliance. With my senses on high alert, I again ordered them to raise their hands. Again, there was movement; however, I still could not see the young man's hands. Keep in mind, I know there is a gun in the rear seat and I'm trying to watch three individuals. Needless to say, someone failing to comply with the order to raise their hands is a problem. The possibility that the individual did not have hands didn't cross my mind!

Looking more intently and shining my flashlight directly on the driver, I realized the young man did not have any hands. He had an arm about six inches long on the left and one about four inches long on the right. I advised the three to keep their hands up and I moved to the passenger side and retrieved the gun, which was loaded with the safety off. Keeping an eye on the offenders, I placed the gun in my truck and then returned to the driver. I got him out of the car and brought him to the front of my truck and checked him for any other weapons.

I heard a vehicle approaching and was glad to see it was CEO Johnson. I told him they had shot and I had one gun in the truck. I asked him to check for any other weapons and to get the other two individuals out and pat them down.

Finding no more weapons I decided we needed to get out of the highway so I told the driver to get back in the car and to pull it around behind the church. Once we had all three vehicles behind the church we quickly ascertained the driver was eighteen years old, the front seat passenger was seventeen, and the rear seat passenger was fifteen.

Having juveniles involved changes how we handle things. It has always been a pain to deal with juveniles; however, it's just the way it is. We got the number for the parents and I called and told them we needed them to come to our location. I have always tried to handle that type of phone call as professionally as possible and with compassion. I know the thoughts that would go through my mind if I were to receive a call from law enforcement in the middle of the night. The first thing I would do was tell the parent I wanted them to know that their child was okay. I would then explain the situation and ask if they could come to our location. After every kid began to have a cell phone, I would normally have the child to call the parent and tell them they were okay but there was someone else they needed to speak with. I would take the phone and explain the situation. Luckily, we were able to get in touch with these kids' parents and got them en route to our location.

I had the driver of the vehicle in my truck. CEO Johnson had one juvenile in his vehicle and the other juvenile remained in the violator's car. I advised the driver of his rights and had him sign a copy of the Miranda warning. I asked him to tell me what had occurred. He stated they had seen a deer and the front seat passenger had shot at it. I asked who the gun belonged to and he said it belonged to his cousin, who lived in Florida. I wrote out a statement exactly like he had told me and had him to read it. He said it was correct and I had him to sign it. At the end of one of his appendages he had one finger about two inches long. He could hold the ink pen with it and signed without any problem.

After the parents of the two juveniles arrived, we advised them of their rights and had them sign Miranda warning sheets. We questioned the juveniles separately. Both of the stories were identical. I should say they were identical with each other. They were anything but identical to the statement the driver had given me. This is a great example of why you separate folks involved in a violation as quickly as possible.

Each passenger stated they had seen a deer back down the road and the driver had stopped the car and retrieved a gun from the trunk. They said he told them if he saw another deer he was going to shoot it. When they saw another deer, he stopped the car and got out and shot at it. They both said the deer ran off. The driver got back in the car and continued northbound. The driver thought he saw another deer and stopped the car and that was when I pulled up behind them. Seeing me behind them, the driver gave the gun to the front seat passenger and told him to put it under the seat. Since it would not go under the seat, he slid it back beside the door. As I said earlier, despite the fact they had been separated ever since I stopped the car, their stories were exactly the same.

I had left the driver in my truck while we talked with the other participants. It was now time to return to the driver and try to get the truth out of him. I started by just staring at the kid and giving him my disgusted look. After a few seconds of that, I told him he had not told me the truth. He quickly looked away from me. I told him to look at me. He again looked at me and I said, "Buddy, you did not tell me the truth." Once again, he immediately turned away. I again told him to look at me. I reminded him that when I had asked him where the gun was he had told me it was in the back seat. I let that hang in the air for a few seconds before I told him both of his buddies had said it was in the trunk. He immediately replied he had meant it was in the trunk. I quickly asked, "Well how did it get out of the trunk?" He looked at me for a few seconds and then nodded his head yes. I asked what that meant and he said he got it out of the trunk. I asked who shot at the deer and he again nodded his head yes. I again asked what that meant and he again nodded his head. I said, "So you did the shooting?" He replied that he did.

I wrote him another statement and had him sign it. He was arrested for hunting at night and hunting from a public road. The driver's mother had arrived on the scene. I explained the charges to both of them and gave them the court date. He was allowed to sign his bonds and go on his way. The two juveniles were released to family members with no charges. I told CEO Johnson he should write down this story because he would likely never see another case like it.

Prior to court, I went by to see the district judge. There were a couple of reasons for the meeting. First, I wanted to let the judge know about the man's handicap so he would not have questions when he saw him in court. I told him the violator had been accompanied by two juveniles, who had not been charged. I informed him I had ascertained that the young man had not had a hunter education course and I felt he should have one. I also advised him I would like to offer the young man an opportunity to attend a handicapped hunt in the future. However, if he was convicted of hunting at night his hunting privileges would be revoked for three years. The judge asked if I would be happy with a $500 fine on hunting from a public road and requiring him to take a hunter education course, while dropping the other charge. I said that would be fine with me.

The young man and his mother appeared in court. The judge did a good job of explaining the dangerous nature of the offense. He advised he was taking the man's age into account. He then levied the $500 fine and told the young man he would have to complete a hunter education course. He advised that the fines could have been much higher (the minimum on night hunting is $2,000) and told the man he had better thank me. He turned and thanked me and the judge told him he was free to go.

The young man completed the hunter education course and was made aware of the handicapped hunting opportunities in the state. It was once again a case like I had never seen before. However, I left there knowing I still had not seen it all, and that I would keep looking!

Your Lucky Spot

AFTER WORKING AS A certified wildlife biologist and conservation enforcement officer (CEO) for over thirty years, I retired. Prior to my retirement I had spoken with Enforcement Chief Kevin Dodd concerning the possibility of me coming back to work as a part-time game warden. He had said he would be interested in that. However, Chief Dodd retired prior to my retirement. Therefore, I was not sure whether or not that was still an option.

About four months after my retirement, I learned that both of the officers in the county adjacent to mine were being transferred to the Montgomery office, which would leave the county without an officer. I was contacted and asked if I would be interested in working there part-time. I said I would and two months later I was rehired.

In addition to myself, Jinks Altiere was also hired to work part-time in Tallapoosa County. Jinks had begun his career with game and fish as a CEO in the southern part of the state. After several years of chasing outlaws, he transferred to the wildlife section as a regional hunter education instructor. In this position, he handled hunter education classes and instructor training in a third of the state as well as continuing to work law enforcement when possible.

In retirement, Jinks had decided to move closer to his grandchildren, which landed him in Alexander City.

Although I had worked in Tallapoosa County for many years, I did not know it intimately as a game warden needs to. Therefore, Jinks and I spent a lot of time exploring. One of the things we quickly figured out was what we felt would likely be a jam up night hunting spot.

Highway 63 is a major highway that runs through the county. Although it is only a two-lane highway, it gets a lot of traffic. In the southern end of the county, the highway passes through an area known as Russell Lands.

While I haven't researched it, I would bet a dollar against a donut the Russell family is one of the largest landowners in the county. You probably have heard of the Russell Corporation, Russell Mills, Russell Apparel, or Russell Land. Russell is a well-known name in Tallapoosa County.

In 1902 Ben Russell founded Russell Athletic as the Russell Manufacturing Corporation in Alexander City. The tiny factory had ten sewing machines and eight knitting machines. While they began making a knit shirt for women and children, they eventually grew and became a major manufacturer of uniforms for teams and apparel for athletes throughout the United States. Russell Mills was a major employer in Tallapoosa County for decades.

In addition to dominating the apparel industry, The Russell family was also busy developing Lake Martin. Lake Martin is one of the largest man-made lakes in the country. The lake is forty-four thousand acres in size and boast over 750 miles of shoreline. The shoreline is home to thousands of lake homes. Russell Lands handles the real estate and manages several lake communities. It is an impressive outfit.

Russell Lands also manages about twenty-five thousand acres of forest land. Much of the forest borders Highway 63, which cuts through the property and crosses the lake. These holdings are extremely well managed with aesthetics as the major objective. This means the pine stands are thinned and burned as they should be. Many of the stands bordering the highway are thinned to a low basal area which provides what is often referred to as a "parklike" stand. While this is beautiful, it does generate a problem. The open stand provides good visibility of the huge deer herd that resides on the property. When you can see deer from the road in Alabama it creates an opportunity for poachers and the game warden.

It did not take long for Jinks and me to decide Highway 63 was likely to be a night hunting hotspot. The fact that you might see thirty or forty deer standing alongside the road any given night helped us arrive to that decision. After a few trips along the road we had selected a couple of spots where we could monitor the activity on the road without being seen.

We soon learned a couple of important things. One thing was there was a lot of traffic on the highway until about eleven at night. While monitoring the traffic, I was amazed by the speed of the vehicles on the highway. Having lived in an area with a lot of deer for many years, I have hit a few and seen many others who have hit them. While hitting deer is often unavoidable, slowing your speed is one precaution you can take. Evidently most of the folks traveling the highway either had never heard that or just did not believe it. One thing that really got my attention was the number of motorcycles flying up and down the highway. For one thing it was fairly cold to be riding a motorcycle and secondly motorcycles and deer just aren't a good match! Yet I observed motorcycles on the highway many nights.

A high volume of traffic made it difficult for a night hunter to operate. I don't think the chance of someone spotting them was their major concern. I knew many night hunters who had shot deer in people's front yards, in subdivisions and in the middle of small towns. I had witnessed several houses that had been shot in to. However, the ones with a little more sense tried to hide their evil deeds. However, I believe the biggest problem the traffic presented to night hunters was a constant interruption. A night hunter needs to be able to ease down the road and stop without other vehicles coming along and disturbing everything. Therefore, we surmised that the hunting would be better after the traffic abated.

However, there was another problem with the area. The stretch of road we felt would be best to work was about four miles long and had two houses along it. Evidently these folks were like many others in that to the best of my knowledge, neither one of them ever called in a complaint of someone shooting. And I know for a fact that folks shot near their houses on numerous occasions. Folks not reporting shooting at night was a major factor that kept our apprehension rate low.

Many years ago, I watched a special on television that was entitled *Wildlife Wars*. It was an account of an undercover operation into illegal deer hunting. The results were incredible. One of the things reported that really got my attention was when the fellow stated that during the course of the investigation they had fired hundreds of shots. They had killed deer, day and night, in people's front yards, back yards, side yards, and under security lights and they had received *no* calls reporting the illegal activity! While that is hard to believe, I can believe it. I have caught night hunters who have shot into homes and the homeowner never called anyone!

After only a couple of nights, we decided we were right when we had thought it would be a "later is better" kind of place. The early traffic was heavy and fast. The fact that we were severely limited on hours we could spend working night hunting dictated we make the best use of our time.

Early January at approximately ten minutes after midnight I set up near Russell Farm Church monitoring Alabama Highway 63 South of Alexander City. Jinks was set up approximately a mile and a half south of me at Russell's Crossroads. At 12:45 a.m. I heard a shot to the southwest of my location. Jinks called me on the radio and reported he had just heard a shot from a small-caliber firearm. I told him I had also heard it.

There are two schools of thought when it comes to working night hunting. While younger officers were prone to try and run down shots, the old-school tried-and-true method is to sit still and let the night hunter come to you. This has worked for game wardens for many years. When I first started working night hunting my mentors told me that was how you had to do it. They said you would not do any good chasing shots in the night.

While we caught a lot of night hunters using their method, it was very difficult to hear a shot in the distance and not to move toward it. Over time, I learned if you knew the area well, you could sometimes pinpoint a shot well enough to locate the shooter. This method had some pitfalls. Just because you had heard a shot, that did not necessarily constitute probable cause to stop a vehicle in the area. However, if you could articulate that there were no other vehicles in the area and could develop probable cause to stop a vehicle, you could make some cases. Having someone shoot in front of you was a much tighter case; however, I had a lot of success moving toward shots and intercepting violators. When you were really lucky, you could move toward a shot and observe the violators shining a spotlight looking for another target.

Although we had both heard a shot, since we neither one could pinpoint it we decided to sit tight. Around one o'clock, I noticed a white Chevrolet pickup as it moved slowly past my location northbound. In a few minutes, I observed the same vehicle going back south. This got my attention. When the driver made the same route again, I felt certain we had something going on.

I radioed Jinks and gave him the description and asked him to watch for the truck. Sure enough, the truck went past his position at a slow rate of speed and turned into the Windemere area. Windemere was a ritzy lake community that was loaded with deer.

In just a few minutes, the truck came back out by Jinks and went south toward the Elmore County line. It was only about a mile to the county line and the Kowaliga bridge. Just in case you aren't from the south and you aren't a Hank Williams fan, you might think that Kowaliga is pronounced cow-a-lig-a. It's not. It is pronounced ca-li-ja. Just so you know.

In just a couple of minutes the truck eased back north past Jinks. It then came by me and proceeded north. As I strained to hear, I could tell the vehicle was turning around at the next intersection. Sure enough, the truck eased back past me. However, this time the truck stopped in the road with his headlights shining off the left side of the road. I knew there were deer at the location where he stopped since other vehicles had been blowing their horns in the area. I waited for the shot I was sure would come. However, the truck pulled away without a shot being fired.

I was certain this truck was hunting but figured he must be looking for a buck. I hated to stop the truck without him having fired a shot, although I felt I could make the case if the driver had a gun. The hunting at night charge is just that, hunting. It does not require that a shot be fired. However, it would be a slam dunk if they did shoot. The driver repeated this activity several times. Patience is essential for a game warden. While I had already observed enough to stop the truck, I knew the wise choice was to wait.

I hated to reveal to the driver that I was observing him. In the event he did not have a firearm, I really didn't have anything. You may be thinking that if he didn't have a firearm then what difference would it make if I stopped him since he obviously wasn't hunting. Well, let me answer that. As I mentioned I had already suspected this guy was looking for a buck to shoot since I knew he had passed on some deer that were alongside the road near my location. The reason I did not want him to know we were observing him was that some night hunters will go out looking without a firearm. When they spot a buck, they will go and retrieve their gun and come back and shoot the deer. If we stop them while they are "just looking" they know we are working the area.

As I was mulling over the best way to address the situation, I had an idea. I remembered that the sheriff's office and Russell Lands security had reported they were having some break-ins in the Windemere area and had asked us to be on the lookout for anything suspicious. Since this truck had repeatedly gone into that area, I felt it would be prudent for the sheriff's office to check the guy out. This way if he did not have a firearm he would not know we were watching him. I contacted Deputy Win Knight and asked if he could assist me by coming to the area and getting the tag number of the vehicle. While he was en route I let him know what was going on and that the vehicle had been in and out of the Windemere area several times in the last hour.

Before the deputy arrived, the vehicle came by me once again. He again stopped with his headlights shining off the roadway. Again, he did not shoot; however, this repeated activity did strengthen my probable cause to stop the vehicle. Within a minute, Win passed my location. I told him the truck was just ahead of him and gave him the description. He told me he was coming up on the slow-moving pickup. Once he was directly behind the truck he said the vehicle had what appeared to be fresh blood on the rear bumper. I asked him to stop the vehicle.

Jinks and I went to his location. Before we arrived, Win called me and said there was a deer in the back of the vehicle. I was elated. I arrived within one minute. The doe appeared to have been shot in the head. The blood coming from its head had not totally coagulated. Seeing how it was now three in the morning, it was obvious to me, having observed literally thousands of freshly killed deer, the deer had been killed after legal hunting hours.

I asked the driver if he had a weapon and he replied he did. I asked where it was and he said in the back seat. I opened the back door and retrieved a Marlin .22 magnum bolt-action rifle with a scope. The gun was loaded. I took the gun and placed it in Jinks's truck.

I asked the driver of the truck, Mick Johnson, to exit the vehicle. I read him the Miranda warning, from a card, and told him I wanted to ask him some questions. I informed him before I asked him anything I wanted him to understand I had been watching him for over two hours. I told him I knew his route, which went from Windermere to County Line Road and then to above the church and back. I let him know I had observed him as he had pulled off the side of the road several times. He simply stared at me with his mouth agape. I advised him I wanted to hear the truth and asked him to tell me what had occurred. He immediately said he had seen the deer (that was now in the bed of his truck) standing on the side of the road and he had shot it. I asked when that happened and he replied, about forty-five minutes ago. While I knew the shot we had heard was two hours earlier, I wasn't going to argue over minor details. I asked him what the role of the other fellow in the truck, Jim Loman, was and he stated he had assisted him in dragging the deer and loading it in the truck. That told me he was an active participant. I knew at this point based on what I had observed and his statement, we would be arresting both men.

I asked Mr. Johnson if he had ever been arrested before and he advised he had. I asked for what and he replied, "Same thing."

I asked where and he replied, "Right here." While I really wanted to, I resisted the strong urge to say, "This must be your lucky place!"

I asked Mr. Loman to exit the truck. I advised him of his rights and asked him to tell me what had occurred. His story was identical to the one Mr. Johnson had given.

We formalized the statements and arrested both men on charges of hunting at night and hunting from a public road. They were also issued a warning for hunting by the aid of a vehicle.

The deer was confiscated and the gun was held as evidence.

The cases were set in the Tallapoosa County District Court. The judge called the defendants to the bench and asked how they pled. They both pled guilty. I had informed the judge that this was a second night hunting offense for Mr. Johnson and therefore it would be a minimum fine of $3,000. The hunting-from-the-road charge carried a $1,000 fine.

Even after going over this with the judge, he charged Mr. Johnson $1,000 on each offense and no cost for a total of $2,000 and gave his gun back. He did revoke his hunting privileges for three years. The codefendant, Mr. Loman, was fined $500 and no court costs on each charge and lost his hunting privileges for three years.

While that is a hard lick, I was disappointed that someone did not receive the maximum punishment for a second offense. I guess he had a second lucky spot!

Such was life when dealing with the court system. You never knew just how it would go. That was our first night hunting case with the judge. It would not be our last. As a matter of fact, it wouldn't be my last encounter with the same truck. But that's another story. See "Knight's First Big Night."

Bambi Kellogg

SOMETHING THAT REMAINED CONSTANT throughout my career, and still today, was folks' obsession with white-tailed deer fawns. While some folks just wanted to keep the deer as a pet, others had other ideas. Such was the case of Bambi Kellogg. In mid-August I received a call from the district officer-in-charge, asking me to contact the Montgomery dispatcher concerning a fawn being held in captivity. In thirty-four years of working with the Wildlife and Freshwater Fisheries Division, I had received this type of call many times. However, this call would turn out to be somewhat different than those in the past.

I must admit there isn't much prettier than a white-tailed fawn. Unfortunately, the beauty of the fawn and the aura of owning a wild animal often proves to be too much temptation for many folks. While some of these people are well intentioned, the truth is the person who picks up a fawn is stealing it from the wild, its mother, and the state of Alabama. Furthermore, their illegal activity often results in the death of the animal.

I will say many people have their heart in the right place. They spot a fawn that can barely walk and they don't see a doe around and they immediately assume the deer has been abandoned. Therefore, they catch the fawn, take it out of its natural environment and away from its mother. They put it in a tote or a dog crate and attempt to feed it some milk. When it doesn't eat and becomes lethargic they call the game warden and tell them they rescued it and need to know what to do with it. That's one scenario. Another is the person who sees a fawn and does their level best to capture it. I have often told folks that the definition of an abandoned fawn is one they could catch. As I said earlier, it normally turns out bad for the fawn.

I contacted the dispatcher and she informed me she had received a call from a lady in New York City—yes, New York City, New York—who had seen a video of an individual holding a fawn in his home on Facebook live. She said the man was in the small town of Jackson's Gap in east-central Tallapoosa County. The dispatcher had viewed the video and provided me with the name of the individual.

I am not "on" Facebook as most folks are. However, my wife has an account and I do need to view something on it from time to time. I had my wife call up the post for me and I watched the video. The man in the video stated the deer was the newest member of his family and he had named it "Bambi." Several times during the video the fawn would "bleat" giving its distress call and the man would comment he was going to have to discipline the deer if it kept doing that. The man was holding the deer haphazardly and I could easily see why someone viewing the video could get upset.

During the course of the day we continued to receive calls from across the country. The video received thousands of views and many comments. The comments ranged from those who thought the deer was cool to those who warned the man it was illegal for him to possess the deer.

Alabama Game and Fish Regulation 220-2-.26 states in part, "Except as authorized by permit issued by the Department prior to the date of this amendment, it shall be unlawful for any person to have in possession any live, protected wild bird or wild animal."

After consultation with my superiors, the decision was made that we should obtain a search warrant before going to retrieve the deer. First thing Monday morning we were waiting at the judge's office. When he arrived, we explained the situation and he immediately authorized a search warrant for the residence. In the meanwhile, we had continued to monitor Facebook for any new developments. It became obvious to us the man was using the deer to gain notoriety. He put on Facebook he was trying to reach one million views on all platforms. We discussed this development with the ADA and asked if he felt Alabama law 9-11-321 would be applicable since the man was obviously using the deer for public exhibition without a permit. The ADA recommended we charge the man with both 9-11-321 and regulation 220-2-.26, which covers the illegal possession of deer.

With search warrant in hand we met with a county deputy and proceeded to the location. The man in the video answered the door and led Sgt. Jerry Fincher to a bedroom where he found the fawn. The man surrendered the fawn and was arrested on both charges. Facts gathered through our investigation prompted us to also arrest his father for possession of a live deer. The deer was taken to a licensed wildlife rehabilitator.

The defendant's defense was one we hear on a regular basis. It was the "they" defense. Many people who are apprehended are quick to inform us that other people, "they" commit the same offense all the time. To me this is akin to a child who has been told no by a parent, saying, "Well, everybody else is doing it!" As you can imagine that defense doesn't carry much weight. Another common response of violators when they are informed their activity is in violation of the law is to ask, "Since when?" In this case, it has been illegal to possess most wild animals in Alabama since 2002. The regulation was promulgated in response to the many problems associated with people possessing live wild animals. Wild animals are meant to be just that, wild.

Interestingly, the defendant videoed the arrests and transmitted it on Facebook live. Both men appeared in Tallapoosa County District Court in September and pled guilty to the charges. District Judge Kim Taylor accepted the guilty pleas and sentenced the men to thirty days in jail, which was suspended on the payment of fines and court costs totaling $1,098.

We felt the judge delivered a strong message that wildlife is meant to be wild. Even though a fawn may appear to be abandoned, the truth is the mother will often move away from their fawns and return later. A white-tailed fawn's best chance of survival is with its mother. Please, leave wildlife in the wild!

More Funeral Security

ONE OF THE BEST ASPECTS of the job of a conservation enforcement officer (CEO) is the unpredictability of what may occur on any given day or night. I cannot count how many times I had a day totally laid out and by the end of the day I had done a little bit of everything except for what I had planned. You had to take the calls as they came and some days they just kept coming.

One mid-February day found Coosa County CEO Drake Hayes patrolling the south end of our rural county along County Road 14 in the vicinity of where he had received a report of a stolen game camera. After the woods became filled with game cameras, it was a very common occurrence for us to receive reports of cameras being stolen. This particular report was a little unique in that the complainant reported the camera was stolen by someone who was riding a motorcycle. The popularity of four-wheelers and side by sides caused a drastic decline in the number of two-wheel motorcycles seen in the woods. Therefore, you can understand how it quickly caught Drake's attention when he met a motorcycle coming down the county road. The fact the rider was not wearing a helmet and the motorcycle did not have a tag did not go unnoticed. He followed the rider, who quickly turned into a driveway. As Drake observed, the fellow quickly got off the bike and ran up on the porch and began knocking on the door. Ironically it was the house of the son of our former game warden.

Drake asked the guy what he was doing and the fellow replied he was going to ask the people in the house if they wanted to buy his motorcycle. When no one came to the door, the officer asked the man to come off the porch. As he stepped off the porch, the officer noticed he dropped something in the shrub. When he asked the man what he had dropped he replied he had not dropped anything. Drake moved over to where the item was dropped and immediately identified it as a glass meth pipe. He ordered the man to get on the ground; however, he refused, saying he had not done anything wrong. In a more forceful tone the officer again ordered the man to get on the ground. Realizing the officer meant business the man lay on the ground and put his hands behind his back. Drake moved in and handcuffed the man and advised him he was under arrest for the possession of drug paraphernalia. He was transported to the county jail.

The next day Drake and I were at the county jail to serve a couple of warrants. (See "A Poor Judge of Distance.") We had a little time before our defendants were supposed to arrive so Drake decided to pull the owner of the meth pipe out of his cell and question him about the game camera. Drake advised him of his rights and told him the reason he was in the area when he had encountered him was he was following up on a report of a stolen game camera. The fellow immediately denied having stolen a game camera. Drake told him the camera had been taken by someone riding a motorcycle and he was the only person he had seen in the area on a motorcycle. Drake then employed a technique I have found to be effective many times. He stared at the man and did not say anything. I have encountered many violators who cannot handle silence. The silence was quickly broken when the man exclaimed, "I didn't steal no camera, I found one." He went on to say he had found a camera on the ground. When asked where the camera was now, he said it was in his mother's van. Calls to the mother were not answered.

The corrections officer told the man he was going to move him to the general population area and the man told him he didn't want to be moved. He was about to learn that you don't usually get your way when you are incarcerated. I was reminded of a sign that had been in the old county jail when I first went to work. It said, "This is not Burger King where you have it your way, this is the county jail and you will do it our way!"

Fast-forward six days. I had a full day planned with no time allotted to Game and Fish. I was suffering from plantar fasciitis and had an appointment with the podiatrist. Before I left the house, I received a call from my partner telling me the district office had contacted him and told him we needed to submit some information concerning complaints received from the past season. My first question was "Isn't that the info we sent last month?" and he replied that it was. That was not unusual. I had learned a long time ago to keep a copy of everything I sent to anybody. Many times, you would receive the same request multiple times. It happens.

Unfortunately, my neighbor, an elderly member of our church, had passed away a couple of days earlier. After returning from my foot appointment, my wife began preparing dishes of food to carry to the church. I don't know about the rest of the country but in the South, when someone dies, we carry food for the family. It is a tradition that our church feeds the family of the lost loved one following the funeral.

I have been a member of a Baptist church since I was six years old. That has been quite a long time. Up until just a few years ago, I would have never believed it would be necessary to have security at church. However, I don't have to tell you that things change. One of the things that has changed at Rockford

Baptist Church is that we now have a security team. The team is led by our retired county sheriff and includes a local police chief, his dad, who is a reserve deputy, myself, and six other men. One of us is scheduled to provide security each time the church doors are open. Duties are rotated on a weekly basis. Although only one man is in effect "on duty," the others are normally there and ready to assist with anything that may come up.

Since I would be attending the funeral, I would be assisting my good friend Robert Smith with security that afternoon and evening. Things such as funerals are a little more difficult to monitor because unlike a regular worship service, where most folks are in the sanctuary, at a funeral you have folks in multiple areas. That is especially true after the funeral when the family is being fed in one area and attendees are scattered about the building. Although we don't think of it in that way, funerals are often very much akin to a family reunion. Therefore, there are people visiting one another throughout the building.

The funeral was nice with many people in attendance. After the graveside service, the family had returned to the church to eat and talk with family and friends.

Things were winding down and many of the people were leaving at approximately 6:00 p.m. I was in the atrium of the church when a young man came in the door and told me I needed to call 911. He stated there was a man outside who needed help. I did not know exactly what the problem was but assumed someone may have fallen or had a medical problem.

I stepped to the door and saw a white male without a shirt and wearing black and white striped prisoner pants standing in the parking lot. I must admit that was not at all what I expected to encounter.

Interestingly, I immediately recognized the man as the fellow who Drake and I had questioned at the jail days earlier. I called the man by his name as I was walking toward him. I told someone else there to call 911 and tell them we needed a deputy immediately.

As I approached, the escaped prisoner began saying he was hurt and needed to go to the hospital. He began to run toward the front of the church and I again called him by name and he stopped. I got hold of his left arm and moved him back toward the church. In order to buy some time, I asked him to tell me what was going on. He said he had fallen in the jail and was hurt but they would not take him to the hospital. He went on to say he was being tortured. I told him to sit down on the ground while still holding onto his arm.

As I helped him down to the ground, he said he did not want an escape charge. He starting trying to get up and I told him to stay on the ground. He told me I wasn't the police and I couldn't hold him. I removed my sheriff's badge from my pocket and showed it to him and told him I was the police. He started trying to get up again and I asked him if he did not remember me talking to him in the jail. He looked at me and with a shocked look on his face he said, "You're the game warden." I said, "Yes I am." About that time, a corrections officer literally came running around the corner of the church. The prisoner was still trying to twist away from me and I asked the officer if he had some cuffs and he removed them from his belt and we handcuffed the man. He was cussing and saying he didn't want an escape charge. I told him he needed to keep quiet and stop struggling or he was going to catch even more charges. He calmed down. Within a couple of minutes, a deputy and another corrections officer arrived on the scene. The prisoner was placed in the back seat of the car and returned to the jail. Of course, he did catch an escape charge.

The man had good reason not to want to be charged with escape. If he had remained in jail until he came to court on the drug paraphernalia charge, he would likely have been released on time served. An escape charge on the other hand is a class C felony and carries a sentence of one year and a day to ten years. The decisions we make carry great consequences. People who play stupid games win stupid prizes.

We all make a lot of choices every day. Some aren't as good as others. What about you? Are you making good choices? I'm not necessarily referring to criminal type situations. Are you making choices that please the Lord? There is one major choice we all make. Do we choose Jesus as our savior? That choice will make all the difference in our lives. Just like in this story, until the Lord comes, everyone will face death. At that point, it will be too late to accept the forgiveness and abundant life that Jesus offers. That choice needs to be made today. Don't wait! God bless.

Smile, You're on OUR Camera

WE ARE OFTEN ASKED EACH HUNTING SEASON what is our most frequent complaint and/or violation. While I'm sure it varies across the state, I'm certain hunting without a permit ranks near the top in most areas. An innovation that has contributed greatly to the number of hunting-without-a-permit calls is the trail camera. Today it is rare that we enter a property that does not have one or more cameras. As a matter of fact, the cameras have proved to be so helpful that we have invested in a few of our own! One well-placed camera generated some photos that culminated in some memorable arrests and convictions.

In the city of Childersburg in Talladega County is an area locally known as the AOW. AOW stood for Alabama Ordnance Works. The AOW was a munitions plant built and operated during World War II. At its peak it produced nearly forty million pounds of munitions per month and employed thousands of people. All operations ceased in 1945. In 1973 the property was designated as excess property. Parts of the property were sold; however, a large amount (2,200 acres) was given to the city of Childersburg for use as an industrial park. Only a small portion has been developed and the remainder has become somewhat of a deer sanctuary. While hunting is forbidden in the area, any area in Alabama that is loaded with deer is going to get hunted and the AOW is no exception. Talladega County game wardens Lt. Jerry Fincher and CEO Greg Gilliland routinely received reports of people hunting in the restricted area. In response to those complaints, Greg had deployed a camera to hopefully get a picture of some of the violators.

A review of the pictures on the camera revealed an individual wearing total camouflage and carrying a long gun entering an area for which he did not possess permission to hunt. The next weekend CEO Gilliland was in the area. Around eight o'clock the officer encountered an individual wearing camo and with no hunter orange visible. The man was carrying a long gun and a telephone. When the poacher stopped to text on his phone, the officer identified himself and told the man to get on the ground. Instead of complying with the command, the man ran, eventually eluding the officer.

CEO Gilliland contacted Lt. Fincher and explained the situation and asked him to come to his location. Since there was not a vehicle on the property, the officers assumed the individual had been dropped out by someone. Therefore, it was likely someone would be attempting to pick up the violator. Lt. Fincher contacted Sgt. Bassett and myself to come to the area to assist. In addition, CEO Kiser was contacted and asked to bring his K-9 to the scene to attempt to track the individual. The officers arrived and set up surveillance in likely areas where someone might attempt to pick up the violator.

From his hiding spot near the main entrance to the property, Lt. Fincher observed a young woman in a small white vehicle as she slowly eased along the roadway. She drove to the gate and turned her vehicle with the passenger side away from the officer. After sitting there for a couple of minutes she started back out of the area. Thinking she may have picked up someone, the lieutenant stepped out and motioned for the driver to stop. He explained he was conducting an investigation and she had driven into a crime scene. He advised her of her rights and asked why she was on the property. She stated she was looking for the home of a friend. He advised her there were no houses on the property. He asked if she was there to pick someone up. She said she was not. He asked what the name of the friend was she was looking for and she said she did not know. I don't know about you, but I don't have a whole lot of friends that I don't know, yet I try to find their house even though I don't know where it is! Obviously, this was interesting and led the officer to probe a little further. He again asked who the woman was there to pick up. She said she wasn't trying to pick up anyone; however, this time it was less convincing than before. After a moment, she added she just wanted to make sure he was okay. Knowing this person was involved in the incident, Lt. Fincher called me and asked me to come to his location.

CEO Kiser arrived with his K-9 and he and CEO Gilliland and Sgt. Bassett began tracking the individual. I arrived at the entrance to the property and met with Lt. Fincher. He quickly explained what had gone on and asked me to speak with the female subject. I introduced myself and Mirandized the young woman and asked her to tell me the story. She did not hesitate. She stated she had brought her boyfriend, Andy Lawson, to the property to hunt deer early that morning. Although she had not planned to pick him up, he had called her and told her the game warden was trying to catch him. Therefore, she had returned to see if she could assist him.

Once we learned the violator's identity, we showed CEO Gilliland a driver's license photo of the suspect and he stated that even though the man was wearing a head cover that concealed his chin and forehead, his eyes and nose were exposed and very distinctive, leaving him convinced it was the same man he had just observed on the property.

Further discussion with the girlfriend allowed us to obtain the suspect's phone number. We also got the phone number for the suspect's father. Based on what we learned, we felt it was likely the suspects father may have picked him up. Lt. Fincher spoke with the father of the suspect and requested to speak with his son. He told Lt. Fincher his son had been with him in Lincoln all day and he would fight "this" in court. This was a very interesting statement in that the lieutenant had not told the man why he wanted to speak with the son!

Learning the young man was no longer in the area, our search was called off. We all gathered up and discussed what had occurred. The K-9 team had located the man's hat and shooting stick, which he had lost while running from CEO Gilliland. The hat contained hair which could possibly be used to verify the hat belonged to the suspect. After a discussion of charges and what would be the next step we all returned to our respective counties.

Since it was obvious the suspect's father was planning to serve as his son's alibi, it was decided we would attempt to obtain the suspect's phone records in an effort to prove the suspect was where we said he was in contrast to what his father was saying.

Obtaining phone records requires a lot of paperwork including subpoenas and search warrants. However, the records often yield a treasure trove of information. In addition to the paperwork, the phone company charges a fee for providing the information. Thankfully the Alabama Conservation Enforcement Officers Association was willing to pay the fee.

I received the records and began the arduous task of working through them. It is truly amazing how many calls and texts some folks send in a single day. The records showed that Mr. Lawson's phone had hit a tower near his home around five in the morning.

It then hit a couple of other towers en route to the AOW. Interestingly, during the time his father claimed he *was with him twenty miles from the AOW, the son's phone was primarily interacting with two towers in the area* for approximately five hours. The phone interacted with one tower 157 times and the other 24 times. A deeper analysis of the data revealed the phone was within approximately two hundred yards of the area where the officer observed the subject. This also coincided with where the young woman said she let Andy Lawson out on the property.

Based on the totality of the circumstances, warrants were obtained for Mr. Lawson for the charges of hunting without a permit, hunting without wearing hunter orange, and fleeing or attempting to elude law enforcement.

Lt. Fincher contacted Mr. Lawson and advised him he held warrants for him. He informed him he would meet with him and allow him to sign his bonds on the charges. The suspect told him he wasn't going to sign anything. Lt. Fincher explained signing the bonds was in lieu of taking him to jail and it was not an admission of guilt. The man repeated that he wasn't going to sign anything. He said he would "just take his chances."

Lt. Fincher and I went to Mr. Lawson's home. We parked out of sight and walked to his house and knocked on the door. After a few minutes, Mr. Lawson came to the door. Lt. Fincher advised him we had obtained warrants for his arrest. He once again told him we would allow him to sign his bond and Mr. Lawson again stated he wasn't going to sign anything. The lieutenant advised him he was under arrest and in a tone that meant business told him to get on his knees. He got on his knees and the lieutenant began applying the handcuffs. Just as this was taking the place, the suspect's father arrived. He immediately exited his car and started toward the lieutenant and his son. I stepped in between them and advised him he needed to stop. He stopped his advance but continued to protest saying we could not arrest his son since he was with him all day on the day the we said he was hunting illegally. I told him we had warrants and his son was under arrest. He then asked if his son could not sign a bond and I told him he was given the opportunity to sign a bond but that he had stated he wasn't signing anything. I advised him we were transporting him to the Talladega County jail and he could bond out from there.

He soon arrived at the jail and went through the volumes of paperwork it takes to place someone in jail. The elder Mr. Lawson was waiting outside and once again protested saying his son couldn't have done this seeing how he was with him.

On March 30, 2021, Mr. Lawson appeared in Talladega County District Court before the Honorable Ryan Rumsey. Lt. Fincher, CEO Gilliland, and I were all present. The judge asked how the man pled to the charge of hunting without a permit. He hesitated for a few seconds and then said, "Guilty." He asked how he pled to the charge of hunting without hunter orange and he replied, "Guilty." He asked how he pled to the charge of attempting to elude and after a few seconds of silence the man replied, "I'm going to plead not guilty to that." The judge told him we would have a trial and told the man to take a seat. The assistant district attorney came over to the officers and said, "Well, I didn't see that coming." He asked if we wanted to go ahead with the trial and we replied we definitely did. He advised he did as well.

The judge called the case and the defendant again approached the bench. The judge asked if he was ready to move forward and he said he would like a court-appointed attorney. The judge explained he would appoint him an attorney; however, if he was found guilty he would have to pay the attorney fees as well. The defendant said he didn't think he could afford that. The judge replied, "Well, it's up to you." The defendant then said, "Well, I did it, I just didn't want it on my record because I was hoping to get a job as a police officer." The judge asked if he was wanting to change his plea to guilty and he said he did.

On the charge of hunting without a permit he was fined $1,000 and court costs. On the no-hunter-orange charge he was fined $50 dollars and court costs. On the charge of fleeing or attempting to elude law enforcement the man was sentenced to fourteen days in jail to be suspended on a fine of $100 plus court costs. He was also placed on twelve months of unsupervised probation.

You never knew how a court case would turn out. I sort of wanted to hear what Mr. Lawson would have to say on the stand. I knew if he and his father would testify they were twenty miles away, it would be difficult explaining how they were so far away while his phone was there on the property with someone actively using it! I hated we didn't get that opportunity; however, I learned a long time ago to take a guilty plea if they wanted to give it!

See Something, Say Something

WHILE WORKING WITH GAME & FISH was a seven-day-a-week job, I did my best not to work on Sunday. The Bible says to remember the sabbath and keep it holy. I did my best to do that. However, it was inevitable that some calls would require attention on the Lord's day.

I had just finished teaching my Sunday School class when I felt my phone vibrating in my pocket. I saw that it was a call from Sgt. Ben Montgomery from Tallapoosa County. Ben had been a conservation enforcement officer (CEO) in Tallapoosa County for about five years prior to being transferred to the Montgomery office. As a matter of fact, he and his partner, Captain Michael East, had both been transferred to Montgomery, which left the county without a game warden. This resulted in my post-retirement employment as a part-time game warden to work in Tallapoosa County.

It was December 17 and the deer season was in full swing. Ben asked me to contact a Tallapoosa County landowner concerning an incident from the night before. I told him I would contact the man as soon as possible.

After church, I contacted Mr. Fred Rayburn in Alexander City and asked what he had going on. He stated he thought someone had shot a deer across the road from his home at about two o'clock in the morning. While I definitely hoped that was something I could do something with, someone "thinking" someone had done something wasn't very strong evidence. I asked if he had in fact seen a deer and he replied that it was lying next to his neighbor's driveway. I asked for his address and told him I would be there as soon as possible.

About forty-five minutes later I pulled up in Mr. Rayburn's driveway. I exited my truck and looked across the road and spotted the white underbelly of a deer. Mr. Rayburn met me on his porch and I asked him to tell me the story. And what a story it was!

The homeowner explained that at approximately 1:45 a.m. he was awakened by the barking of his dog and got up to investigate. As he stood in the dark on his front porch, he observed a small car as it slowly drove past his home. After about a minute, the car returned going in the opposite direction. He explained this was suspicious since traffic was normally nonexistent in his neighborhood at that time of the morning. He decided to maintain his vigil and sure enough in a few minutes he again observed the same vehicle coming down the road in front of his home. This time someone in the vehicle was shining a spotlight out the window. He now surmised they were definitely up to no good and were likely trying to kill one of the deer that frequented the neighborhood.

Within a couple of minutes, the car again came along the road shining the light out the window. The vehicle again went out of sight. However, within two minutes the vehicle returned. As the driver slowly drove along the road, they turned off their headlights and pulled into the driveway across the street from where Mr. Rayburn watched from his porch approximately two hundred feet away. The car stopped and the trunk popped open and both the driver and passenger side doors opened.

Mr. Rayburn explained his neighbor was in the hospital in Birmingham and he feared these people might have known that and were going to break into the neighbor's home. Therefore, he reached inside his front door and turned on his porch light. Oh, what a difference a little light on the situation makes. He said the trunk was immediately slammed shut and the car quickly backed out of the driveway at a high rate of speed.

As they were backing out, Mr. Rayburn was running to his truck. He said he jumped in his vehicle and pursued the small car. While I definitely understand the urge to pursue someone you feel is up to no good around your home, it isn't a very good idea. Chases are often dangerous, and what happens if you were to catch them, which could be much worse?

Mr. Rayburn said speeds reached as high as eighty miles per hour. He said the car was not able to outrun him and interestingly it went to a residence on Highway 63. Not wanting a confrontation, Mr. Rayburn went past the residence and took a position where he could observe. He stated the vehicle, a dark-colored Honda Civic, had pulled in beside the house.

While conducting surveillance on the house and vehicle, Mr. Rayburn contacted the Tallapoosa County Sheriff's Office (TCSO) who dispatched a deputy. Deputy Hotchkiss soon arrived. Mr. Rayburn explained all that had occurred. However, at this time he did not know there was a dead deer lying beside his neighbor's driveway. The deputy told Mr. Rayburn he would go and check the vehicle he had followed and see what he could find out. Keep in mind, it was now about three o'clock in the morning.

Mr. Rayburn returned home and decided to check his neighbor's property to see if he could ascertain whether or not anything was missing. Although he did not think the car had been there long enough for anyone to grab anything, the multiple passes by the vehicle made him think they may have let someone out earlier. When he shined his flashlight on the property he observed the white underbelly of a deer. He investigated and found a dead doe lying approximately ten yards off the driveway. This was directly adjacent to where the car, with its headlights off, had stopped and opened the trunk and doors.

Assuming the deer had been shot, Mr. Rayburn contacted the TCSO who in turn contacted Sgt. Montgomery who in turn contacted me. I told Mr. Rayburn I felt certain the folks had probably shot the deer, which caused his dog to bark, which woke him. They were then coming back with the light trying to see if they could spot the deer. We walked across the road and I examined the deer. It was a large doe that I estimated would weigh approximately 115 pounds live. I found a bullet entry wound on the left shoulder. The size of the wound indicated it was a small-caliber bullet. There was no exit wound.

Mr. Rayburn said he had checked the residence where he had chased the car to a couple of hours earlier and it was still there. I asked him if he would write a statement containing everything he had told me. He said he would. I told him I would take things from here and I would be back in touch with him.

I left his residence and went to the location on Highway 63. There I observed the vehicle he had described parked just as he had stated. However, the license plate had been removed from the vehicle. Now while I'm not the sharpest knife in the drawer, the fact the tag had been removed from the vehicle seemed to me to be an incriminating development. Of course, I'm suspicious of everybody.

Thinking back on all the information I had gathered, I theorized that the folks in the car were night hunting on the Creek Road and shot a deer with a small-caliber rifle. The shot caused Mr. Rayburn's dog to bark waking the landowner. The night hunters left the area and then returned to retrieve the deer. On their first pass they failed to spot the deer. They soon returned shining with a spotlight in an attempt to locate the deer. After three passes with the spotlight, they spotted the deer's white stomach lying just off of the driveway of the residence across the road from Mr. Rayburn's residence. To escape detection, they turned their headlights off and pulled in the driveway to a position approximately ten yards from the dead deer. Keep in mind the deer was less than a hundred feet from the neighbor's house. They opened the trunk and got out to retrieve the deer. Seeing the porch light come on across the street, they reentered the car and took off at a high rate of speed and evidently went straight to their house with the neighbor in pursuit.

My next move was to speak with the deputy who had gone to the residence that night. I contacted the TCSO dispatcher and asked if Deputy Hotchkiss was on duty. She advised he should be at the office in a couple of hours. I asked her to let him know I would like to meet with him about the call from the Creek Road the night before.

I met with Deputy Hotchkiss and told him I was following up on the incident from the previous night. I advised him I had a strong suspicion that the people that Mr. Rayburn had thought were breaking into his neighbor's house were actually night hunting. He told me that made more sense than what they had told him. He said when he went to the residence on Highway 63, Mr. Jeff Cosgrove had answered the door. He noted Mr. Cosgrove was wearing a hunting type knife on his belt and appeared to be intoxicated. The deputy asked Mr. Cosgrove if he had been on Creek Road earlier and he confirmed he had. When asked about pulling into the driveway of a residence and opening his trunk he replied he was changing a flat tire. When asked about shining a light, Mr. Hooks stated they did shine a flashlight while changing their tire. When the deputy asked who was "they" he replied his girlfriend was with him. A warrant check revealed Mr. Cosgrove

137

had a warrant for domestic violence and he was arrested and transported to the Alexander City jail. The deputy told me he could make me a copy of the bodycam footage of his encounter and I told him that would be great.

Now I had the name of at least one suspect. Thinking about what the deputy had said, I speculated Mr. Cosgrove had called his accomplice and advised them to remove the license plate from the car. I knew I could probably get a tape of the phone call; however, I did not think it would be necessary since Mr. Cosgrove had admitted to the deputy that he was on Creek Road shining a light and was followed home by Mr. Rayburn who never lost sight of the vehicle.

The interview by Deputy Hotchkiss placed Mr. Cosgrove at the scene where the deer was shot and killed. He did not deny shining the light, stopping in the driveway beside the deer, and opening his trunk. I felt his assertion that he was changing a tire was untrue seeing how a NASCAR pit crew would be hard pressed to change a tire that quickly.

I ran Mr. Cosgrove through our criminal database and was not surprised to find he had a previous conviction for hunting at night, hunting from a public road, and hunting by the aid of a vehicle six years earlier. In addition, it revealed he was a convicted felon and was on probation for manufacturing methamphetamine.

I followed up with detectives from the Alex City Police Department (ACPD) and the Tallapoosa Sheriff's Office. I also spoke with pardons and parole officers and the assistant district attorney. In most cases when someone is on probation or parole, their parole officer can search their residence without a warrant at any time. It was decided myself and others would accompany the probation officer to the residence the next morning and interview Mr. Cosgrove.

CEOs Ben Montgomery and Johnny Johnson Jr. and I met with Probation Officer Jason Smith and discussed our plan. We also spoke with the assistant district attorney. Since the residence was in the Alexander City jurisdiction, we contacted ACPD and advised them what was going on. All of the agencies were familiar with Mr. Cosgrove seeing how he was a frequent client with each group.

Arriving at the residence, I went to the front door and CEO Johnson went to the rear. Before I knocked on the door, I heard Sgt. Montgomery giving some loud verbal commands to someone off to the south. I moved back off the porch and spotted an individual, wearing camouflage and carrying a rifle, coming out of the woods. It was Mr. Cosgrove.

CEO Montgomery was moving toward him and confronted him. CEO Montgomery took his rifle and escorted him to my vehicle and told him to put his hands on the hood of my truck. I took the .243 Remington rifle and placed it in my truck. I moved over to Mr. Cosgrove and removed a knife from his belt. I read him the Miranda warning.

CEO Montgomery asked the man if he had a permit to hunt on Russell Lands property. He stated he did not. Ben pointed at the property the man had just walked off of and asked if that wasn't Russell Lands property. There was no answer. CEO Johnson had observed where the man was on the property and had walked over to take a look. He soon returned with a handful of corn indicating the property was baited. CEO Montgomery asked if he possessed a hunting license and he shook his head no.

With everything under control, ACPD Officer Smith and I entered the house and checked for any other weapons. The house was occupied by Mr. Cosgrove's mother and father. I had run a check on them earlier and had discovered Mrs. Cosgrove had a conviction for possession of meth precursors. These are items used to "cook" meth. In the residence, we located items consistent with the manufacture of methamphetamine in Jeff's room. We contacted the Tallapoosa County Drug Task Force and asked them to come to our location.

We secured the residents and left an ACPD officer with them. We moved back outside and waited on the task force to arrive. While waiting we decided to question Mr. Cosgrove concerning the previous night hunting incident. The interview began as many do with the suspect claiming no knowledge of what we were talking about. Seeing how he was a convicted felon, I had anticipated he might be a difficult interview. However, I had several things in my favor. I began by stating a few facts. I told him that although my primary concern was the night hunting incident and the illegal hunting we had observed as we drove up, I had also noticed some damning evidence inside the residence that would probably make it tough on anyone with past felony drug convictions. I hoped he would be smart enough to realize that it wasn't only his freedom that was at stake. I could tell the statement had gotten his attention, but he was still reluctant to admit to the night hunting.

As he sat in a chair in the yard, I went to my truck and retrieved the knife I had taken off his side earlier. I walked back to where he was sitting with the knife in my hand. He was doing his best to keep up his tough guy persona but it was about to become more difficult. Although I wasn't positive about what I was about to say, I felt it was a really good bet. I asked the man, "Is this the same knife the deputy took from you the other night when he took you to jail?" He had not anticipated that question, which was what I had hoped. He stammered around and eventually said, "Yeah." That was what I was looking for. I immediately followed up with, "Wasn't that when you told him you had been on Creek Road that night?"

140

He looked at me with a look of total defeat and I knew it was over. He confessed he had been night hunting on Creek Road and had shot a deer there. He stated he shot it with a .22 rifle. He said he was accompanied by his girlfriend, Bonnie Lynn Ricks, and Les Simon. He stated he had shot the deer and came back home to get another light to use to look for it. He gave a very detailed statement.

The drug task force arrived and searched the house. A meth lab was found in Jeff's room and another was located by CEO Johnson on the Russell Lands property where Mr. Cosgrove had been hunting.

Mr. Cosgrove was charged with hunting at night and hunting from a public road and issued a warning for hunting by the aid of a vehicle for the night hunting incident. He was charged with hunting without a permit, hunting by the aid of bait, and hunting without a license and issued a warning for hunting without hunter orange for the incident near his house. In addition, he was charged with possession of a controlled substance, possession of drug paraphernalia, and first-degree manufacturing of methamphetamine, a felony. He was taken into custody by the drug task force and transported to jail.

I reviewed available data and eventually came up with a local address for the alleged accomplice Mr. Les Simon. Mr. Simon was contacted by his probation officer and asked to come into the office on the following Wednesday. CEO Johnson and I were waiting when he arrived. We advised him of his rights and asked him to tell us what had occurred. He did not hesitate. His statement closely resembled that of Mr. Cosgrove. He explained that Bonnie Ricks was driving to begin with and Mr. Cosgrove had shot a deer. After that Mr. Cosgrove had got behind the wheel and allowed Mr. Simon to shoot a deer. They then returned home and swapped vehicles and left their gun at home to go back and retrieve the deer. When they had stopped to retrieve the deer Mr. Cosgrove had shot, someone came up behind them and they hurriedly left the area.

We took a written statement from Mr. Simon and obtained warrants for his arrests for hunting at night and hunting from a public road. He was also arrested for procurement of meth precursors (felony), conspiracy to commit methamphetamine manufacturing and a felony probation violation.

Seeing how we had been unable to get Mr. Cosgrove to reveal where the rifle they had used was, we asked Mr. Simon about it. He insisted the rifle used, a .22-caliber semiautomatic rifle, was borrowed from the next-door neighbor of Mr. Cosgrove.

After receiving statements from Cosgrove and Simon, I spoke with Assistant District Attorney Kevin Hall concerning obtaining warrants for Bonnie Ricks for hunting at night and hunting from a public road. He agreed that would be appropriate and I obtained the warrants.

Several attempts to locate Ms. Ricks were unsuccessful. I continued to try to find a way to contact the woman about the warrants. Eventually I was able to get a possible phone number for her. I called the number and an older woman answered the phone. I advised her who I was and that I needed to speak with Bonnie Ricks. She explained she was Ms. Ricks's mother. She told me her and her daughter were currently at the Tallapoosa County jail visiting Mr. Jeff Cosgrove. I advised her to stay there and I would be there momentarily.

I called CEO Johnson and asked him to be en route to the jail. We each arrived approximately fifteen minutes later. I found Ms. Ricks sitting in an orange Dodge Dakota pickup with her mother. I introduced myself and asked her to come and sit in our truck. She sat in the passenger seat with me in the driver's seat and CEO Johnson in the backseat. I felt it was very important that CEO

Johnson be able to observe what went on seeing how this was his first year working as a CEO. In addition, it was always best to have someone else present when you questioned a female.

I began by advising Bonnie of her rights and had her to sign a Miranda warning sheet. I asked if she knew what we wanted to talk about and she indicated that she did. Seeing how we were sitting outside the jail and she was there visiting the man we had arrested for hunting at night, I felt pretty certain she knew what was up. I asked her to tell me what had occurred on the night in question. She did not hesitate.

She said Mr. Cosgrove and Mr. Simon had gone to the MAPCO convenience store and had stayed gone for an hour and a half. When they returned they told her they needed her to drive them somewhere in her car. She stated she drove where they told her to. It was a one way in and out road. She said she was really mad at Cosgrove and she stopped the car and they were arguing when someone came up behind them and they took off. The vehicle followed them back to their house. Shortly thereafter a sheriff's deputy arrived and arrested Cosgrove on a warrant.

It rarely failed that when you questioned multiple subjects involved in the same incident each one would shade the facts of what occurred to make them look less guilty. I advised her that much of what she had told me sounded familiar; however, I felt she had left out much of what had gone on. She did a poor job of acting surprised. I asked her to go over the statement again. She went through it again and added a couple of details. I sat there and just let things hang in the air for a minute. I asked her to go over it again. I could tell she really didn't appreciate having to tell it again. Of course, I did not care whether she liked it or not. I was trying to get to the truth. She told the story again. However, she was now having difficulty keeping it straight. She added another detail or two. I asked if she was aware that Mr. Simon had already been arrested and had given me a detailed statement of what had occurred. You could tell this put a lump in her throat as she said she did not know that. I allowed that to resonate for a minute.

I again pressed her on her statement. Eventually, she admitted she had driven Cosgrove and Simon back to the area in an attempt to retrieve a deer they had shot. They had told her where to stop and Cosgrove had popped the trunk open and he and Simon had got out to get the deer. They were startled by lights coming on across the street. They took off and a vehicle from across the road followed them back to Cosgrove's house. This obviously meshed perfectly with the information I had received from the homeowner earlier.

I advised Ms. Ricks that based on her involvement, I had obtained warrants for her arrest and I was placing her under arrest for hunting at night and hunting from a public road. I advised her that the deer being shot in the yard of a home was extremely dangerous and she stated she understood. I also issued her a warning for hunting by the aid of a vehicle. I then explained the vehicle used could possibly be confiscated. She explained the car, a black Honda Civic, had belonged to her stepfather, who had recently passed away. She added that the tag on the vehicle had expired. That statement jogged my memory and I asked her who had taken the tag off the car on the night of this incident and she replied that Jeff Cosgrove had removed the tag.

I explained when her court date was and she replied she already had to be in court on that date for another charge concerning missing money from her past employer.

Seeing how Cosgrove and Simon had felony charges, the misdemeanor hunting cases took a back seat in the court system. Therefore, Ms. Ricks's cases were heard prior to the men's cases. She pled guilty and received fines and court costs totaling over

$3,000. Months later, Cosgrove and Simon pled guilty and received fines and court costs totaling thousands of dollars. They were returned to prison on their probation violations.

Had a concerned neighbor not have called the sheriff's office about some suspicious activity, none of these cases would have been made. The callers' information and a follow-up investigation resulted in ten misdemeanor arrests, four misdemeanor warnings, and six felony arrests. That's twenty charges!

It is impossible to know how many folks get by with illegal hunting activity simply because people who know about it will not call and report them. Something the complainant mentioned to me on the first day I spoke with him stuck in my mind. He said he would have to come up with an answer for his five-year-old daughter who loved to watch the deer in their yard for why the deer wasn't there anymore. I told him I was sure another deer would probably move into the area. However, it is sad to think that you have to try and explain to your innocent child how some bad people with no regard for the wildlife resource or the people living in your neighborhood had driven by in the middle of the night and shot a deer within one hundred feet of your neighbor's house. When you think about it, we should have gone for thirty charges!!!

My friend Terry Grosz said wildlife dies without making a sound. That is true. However, you have a voice. If you know of illegal hunting activity, contact your state wildlife agency. Most departments have a toll-free tip line for information. Remember, these poachers are stealing from you and the next bullet may come through your window!

I Might See a Big Buck

WHILE THE ADVENTURES IN THE FIELD were often wildly entertaining, the adventures in the courtroom were nothing to sneeze at. You never knew what someone would say or do. It often made for some interesting theater.

I was in the south Talladega district court for a case I and others had put a boatload of time on to be heard. Other game wardens present included Lt. Jerry Fincher, Sgt. Jason Bassett, and CEO Greg Gilliland. We had all been present on a hunting-without-a-permit and eluding-an-officer incident and had finally got the matter before the court. However, there were several other cases on the docket as well.

As District Court Judge Ryan Rumsey worked through the docket, he came to a young man named Joey Kelly who had been charged with hunting from a public road. The judge called the young man to the bench and advised what he was charged with and asked how he pled. The defendant answered, "Not guilty." Judge Rumsey instructed the officer and the defendant to raise their hands and be sworn. He asked Greg to tell the court why the man had been charged.

Greg testified as he was driving along the public road in the Talladega National Forest he observed a vehicle sitting on the side of the road with the door open. Whenever we saw something like that we immediately suspected someone had made a quick

146

exit probably to do something illegal. Hey, it's just the way we are wired. As the officer got closer, he observed a man walking up the road in front of the vehicle. He described the man as walking in sort of a crouch with his rifle in his hands as if he was stalking something. Greg stated he pulled in behind the car, exited his truck and walked toward the individual. The man, who appeared to be actively scanning the woods, eventually turned and saw Greg standing behind him. The officer identified himself and casually asked what the man was doing. He replied he was looking at some trails. Greg asked if he could examine the man's rifle and he handed it to him and cautioned, "It's loaded." Greg said he told the man walking the public road with a loaded rifle and peering into the woods constituted hunting from the road. The hunter protested he wasn't hunting he was just checking out the area. Greg again advised him he did not need his loaded rifle just to check out the area. He told him someone walking the road and checking out trails with a loaded rifle in hand was hunting from the road. He issued him a citation.

The judge asked the defendant if he would like to ask the officer any questions and he said he would not. The judge asked the fellow if he was in fact hunting and replied he was not. The defendant stated he was just walking along and looking at some trails where he thought he might want to come back and hunt. The judge asked if his gun was loaded during this incident and he said it was. The judge asked why his gun was loaded if he was just looking at some trails. The guy hemmed and hawed around a little bit and didn't answer. The judge said, "Can you answer that?" and the fellow replied, "Well I might have seen a big buck down in there on one of those trails."

As happened many times during my career, it was all I could do not to laugh out loud! Based on his testimony, the judge found the fellow guilty. The judge advised his fine would be $1,000 plus court costs and he would give him some time to pay it off if he needed it. The guy immediately told the judge he couldn't pay a fine like that. He continued saying he owed fines in a bunch of other counties and there was no way he could pay this fine. The judge advised him he would allow him to set up a payment plan and he would allow him to set the amount he would pay monthly. The defendant continued to protest saying he could not afford to pay the fine. The judge had heard enough and asked him if he could afford to sit in jail for thirty days instead. The fellow was extremely frustrated and loudly asked, "Well how much do I have to pay a month?" The judge reminded him he had already told him he would allow him to set the monthly payment; however, he better set an amount he could pay each month since in the event he failed to pay he would be picked up and placed in jail. The fellow was still upset and again told the judge he owed a lot of fines in other counties. The judge had heard enough and told him he wasn't worried about other counties and asked if he was going to set an amount or go to jail. The defendant said he could pay twenty dollars a month. The judge told him at that rate he should have it paid off in just over five years!

I must admit I found it an interesting defense that you owed so many fines in other counties you couldn't afford to pay the judge who you were standing in front of. I knew he was lucky he wasn't standing in some of the other counties I worked in! I guess he's lucky he didn't see a big buck standing on one of those trails!

Can You Bring Me
Some Printer Paper?

A LOT OF THINGS HAVE CHANGED in law enforcement during the past thirty-seven years. If you've read many of my stories you've probably come across one that referred to me getting a radio call from the Montgomery office telling me to go to a telephone and call them. When I arrived in Rockford, the county seat of Coosa County, there was a pay phone in the Majik Mart convenience store parking lot at the corner of Alabama Highway 22 and US Highway 231. I don't know if there are any pay phones in the state today. If you had told me that before I ended my career I would be able to sit in my truck and check for warrants, check vehicle registration, and view someone's list of current licenses I would have had a hard time believing it. To help you understand that, we did not have E911 addresses until about nine or ten years ago and it still isn't 100 percent accurate!

Our county has about ten thousand residents scattered across 652 square miles, which is about a thousand people less than when I began my career. That evidently isn't the type of area where cell phone service providers flock to. Add in the fact that our topography often resembles any roller coaster you've ever ridden on, and you can guess our cell service isn't the best. That is not to say we don't have cell towers scattered across the county.

Thirty-seven years ago, when I arrived in Coosa County, the Coosa Wildlife Management Area (WMA) was known as one of the darkest areas in Alabama. Having worked many nights on the WMA I can tell you it was as dark as the inside of a black cat. There were many spots on the thirty-eight-thousand-acre area where you could not see a light in any direction. Today, there are few, if any, places on the area where you can go that you do not see the flashing lights atop multiple towers. I liked it better dark.

While we don't have all the bells and whistles like some big-city departments, we have advanced exponentially in the area of technology. That is true with the Department of Conservation and the Coosa County Sheriff's Office (CCSO) who I work with on a regular basis. One of the advances I never thought about was actually having a computer printer in my vehicle. Keep in mind the first home printer I ever had was about two feet wide and one and a half feet deep. Obviously, that would have been difficult to mount in the cab of my truck. If you have ever looked inside a law enforcement vehicle, one thing you likely noticed was there wasn't very much extra space. That was especially true in our vehicle in that it often served as our office as well. I often commented that all I had in the cab of my truck would barely fit in the bed of the truck and that wasn't a tremendous exaggeration. I had everything from extra clothing to food to departmental paperwork to three hundred keys. It was pretty cramped.

Such space limitations called for creativity to be able to fit everything in. One pretty neat innovation was the development of the headrest printer. Yes, the passenger side headrest housed a printer inside of it. The printer itself was very small and the majority of the space was needed for a roll of printer paper. The roll of paper was tightly compressed and when it printed in looked like the receipt you receive from a gas pump except it was about eight inches wide. Again, if you would have told me when I started I would eventually punch a button on the computer in my truck and it would spit out a ticket, I would have been hard to convince.

Recently while working with the CCSO we teamed up with the Goodwater Police Department to conduct a roadblock in the Goodwater jurisdiction. I was about to learn I wasn't the only one who wasn't totally familiar with the latest and greatest technology. We had just got our vehicles in place when the first car came through. You never know whether or not a roadblock in our rural area will be productive. On this night the driver of the first vehicle stopped did not have a driver's license or insurance on the vehicle. The Goodwater Police officer went to his vehicle and began typing the violations into his computer. One of the problems with sharing a vehicle with other officers soon became evident when the officer learned his printer was out of paper. The officer was certain there would be another roll of paper in either the glove compartment or the trunk of the car. Unfortunately, he was mistaken. As fate would have it, there was not an extra roll of paper in any vehicle on the scene.

Frustrated the officer returned to the stopped vehicle and inquired as to whether or not the passenger had a license. She did. He told the current driver she would need to let the passenger drive and this would be her lucky night and neither of them needed to drive the car again until they obtained insurance for it.

The officer returned to his unit and radioed his dispatcher. He knew the dispatcher's shift was ending and they would be coming past us shortly. He asked if she would bring him some printer paper when she came by. She advised she would. Only a couple of vehicles had passed through prior to the dispatcher rolling up on the scene.

The officer walked up to the window and the dispatcher handed him a short stack of paper, about fifty sheets, she had taken out of the printer at the station. I almost bit a hole in my lip trying to keep from laughing. The look on his face was not a happy one. It was more of a what am I supposed to do with this! I'm sure the dispatcher had never been in a patrol car and never thought about it needing a different type of paper.

While training our new young officer, I was once again reminded how things have changed. While discussing how sometimes a day that seems the same can be totally different, I commented that although the situation is a carbon copy of one you had previously, it may turn out totally different. It was obvious he did not understand what I was saying. He asked what kind of day I had referred to. I repeated it was a carbon copy. I must admit I felt a little old when he asked, "What's a carbon copy?"

It always helped to have something humorous happen to balance out the stress of being in law enforcement. Of course, being repeatedly reminded I was old as dirt wasn't that funny!

For All You Know That Guy Is a Game Warden

IN MY MOTHER'S LAST YEARS, more than once she shared with me that getting old wasn't for sissies! I was fortunate to have both of my parents well into adulthood. Unfortunately, a combination of Parkinson's and old age took my dad. My mother lived almost another six years before she succumbed to Alzheimer's. It was a difficult time. Alzheimer's is a cruel disease that unfortunately runs in my family.

Three months prior to my mother's passing, I took over the care of my first game warden partner, Hershel Patterson. After a series of falls he had to move into assisted living. I became his caregiver, which generated nearly weekly trips to a doctor's office. During this time, I was working as a part-time game warden. Our part-time officers were officially labeled as Special Task Force and unofficially referred to as the Old Geezer Squad! The unit was made up of officers who had retired and come back on a part-time basis. I enjoyed the work and it continued to be a great source of stories!

In 2022 Hershel developed a problem that resulted in several trips to the gastroenterologist and eventually to the hospital for a colonoscopy. That trip turned out to be pretty interesting.

We had arrived at the hospital early that morning and handled all of the registration paperwork. They eventually took him back for the procedure and my wife and I were escorted to a waiting room. The chairs in the waiting area were positioned so they formed sort of a square. Always the law enforcement officer, I selected a spot with my back to the wall and a good view of the rest of the room.

The area was not crowded and eventually four folks sat down across from us. It appeared to me there was an elderly woman with her son who appeared to be retired military and probably in his fifties. Sitting near them were two other women who were probably around forty years old. At this time, the hospital was still requiring that everybody wear a mask, which made it a little difficult to get a good description.

The folks across from us were talking and I heard the fellow tell one of the ladies that when he finished up there he was going to go to his second job. She asked, "What's that?" He chuckled a little and replied, "Fishing." She immediately told him she would like to have some fish and asked him if he would sell her some. He immediately told her she shouldn't say stuff like that. Then he pointed at me and said, "For all you know that guy's a game warden!" She said, "Is he really the game warden?" and the guy said he didn't know but you had to be careful what you say. It was a good thing I had a mask on since otherwise they would have seen my mouth hanging open in disbelief! To the best of my knowledge I had never seen the guy before and I was sure he could not have recognized me with the mask on!

The man went on to tell her that you had to be careful what you said or put on Facebook because if the game warden saw it he could come and give you a ticket. He cautioned that if you put something on Facebook you needed to put "we" caught these fish. That way the game warden didn't know how many of you there were. He told her the limit on crappie was thirty but if you had a picture of sixty on Facebook and you said we caught them then the game warden didn't know how many you had caught. I leaned over and told my wife that before we left I was going to show him my badge and ask him to give me a call if he ran across anybody selling fish. Unfortunately, a nurse came and got him and his mother and took them out of the room.

Thinking about that reminded me of a story our former undercover guy had shared with me. This officer had worked undercover details all over Alabama and throughout the United States. I loved to listen to his stories, some of which would definitely curl your hair! I remember him telling me about working in northeast Alabama in an effort to catch some of the folks that were hunting bears illegally. We did not and still don't have a black bear season, although our number of bears has been increasing. At this time there were few bears but evidently enough that some unscrupulous souls were doing their best to kill one. The officer told me he was in the area in an undercover truck posing as a deer hunter and hoping to encounter some of the wrongdoers.

I'm certain you have heard the adage that it's better to be lucky than good. I don't know that I believe that, but I will admit there seemed to be a lot of luck involved in many of our cases. When you were trying to cover 652 square miles, there had to be some luck involved in your being in the right place at the right time. Of course, I also know the harder I worked the luckier I got!

Our officer said as he slowly rounded a curve on the mountainous road he noticed a pickup with a dog box on the back stopped in the roadway with two guys in camo standing beside it and a dog standing on the dog box. He said it was sort of a Mutt and Jeff situation with one of the guys being maybe five feet six inches short and the other about six feet six inches tall. He eased to a stop and exited his truck and approached the men. He greeted them by saying he had been up there all morning and had not seen as much as a deer track. He said it was obvious the guys weren't in the mood to talk; however, he pressed forward. He asked the guys if they had had any luck and received a very gruff "No." He again stated he had not even seen a deer track and wondered if there were even any deer in the area. He said the guys were making it blatantly obvious they didn't want to talk; however, he had the gut feeling he really needed to engage them so he kept trying. He asked, "Have y'all killed any deer up here?"

While the tall guy remained silent, in an aggravated tone, the shorter one barked, "We ain't deer hunting!" Our officer gave a confused look and said, "You ain't?" The aggravated man replied, "We're bear hunting!" Our guy gave a startled look and said, "I didn't know there were bears up here." The man replied there were bears up there, their dog was a bear dog, and that's what they were hunting. Doing his best to play dumb, the officer said, "I didn't know you could hunt bears up here." The fellow quickly replied, "You can't!" and told him that was why they needed him to move on. Although he felt he had all he needed to make the case for illegally hunting bears, the officer decided one more piece of information would cinch his case up tight. He asked the fellow, "Are you not afraid the game warden will get you?" He said the guy scoffed and said, "They ain't no game wardens up here." As the officer locked eyes with the man he said he could see the wheels turning in his head and watched as his expression changed. In a not-so-belligerent tone the man looked at the officer and said, "You ain't?" The officer replied, "Yes, I am."

After an awkward pause, the guy regained his composure and told the officer he was only joking, to which the officer replied, "I'm not."

Mr. Joe Still Shooting at Seventy-Six

SOME HABITS DIE HARD. During my career I've known several folks I would categorize as old-timers who I have apprehended. Of course, what constitutes an old-timer has changed over time. A few years ago, the two young wardens in my county got a call from a hunting club member who explained they had found a wallet outside their clubhouse and it did not belong to anyone in their club. They met with the club member who felt it must belong to someone who was illegally hunting on the property. They called me and gave me the name from the license in the wallet and asked if I was familiar. The name didn't ring a bell so I asked how old the individual was and they replied that he was pretty old in that he was born in 1965! I responded, "Do you think he's still able to walk?" Seeing how that is a few years younger than me. However, I remember when I thought the forty- and fifty-year-olds I was catching were old. I don't think that anymore!

Lt. Jerry Fincher had called me and reported that an old violator was once again plying his trade in Talladega County and asked if I would assist him in catching the culprit. I told him I would be happy to do that. We deployed my turkey decoy and the suspect drove right past it several times without giving any indication that he had spotted it.

157

This violator had the same problem that plagued many outlaws: he could not keep his mouth shut. He enjoyed visiting the local café and crowing about the deer and turkey he had killed from the road. Some of the patrons took exception and had contacted Jerry with complaints.

Not only was this guy abusing the resource, where he was plying his craft was very problematic and dangerous. The area that the ne'er-do-well was driving almost every day was Shocco Springs Road. Shocco Springs is a Christian conference center where, in a normal year, may have as many as twenty thousand visitors. Not only are there people in the many buildings, there are also numerous walking trails through the woods. Obviously, someone shooting indiscriminately from the road creates an extremely hazardous situation. Many people who hear of someone hunting illegally only consider that they may take an animal. They rarely think about the fact that someone shooting from the road puts many people in danger. Unfortunately, many judges and prosecutors don't understand that either. Thankfully, for the most part, judges I have worked with live in the country and have witnessed incidents that help them to understand the seriousness of violating our laws.

As we once again neared the deer season, our violator, who we will refer to as Joe, resumed making his daily excursions through the Shocco area. The complaints again started rolling in and we set up a detail to try to apprehend Joe. I told Jerry I would get with CEO Greg Gilliland and we would go and prepare a spot to deploy the stuffed wonder. I called Greg and asked if he had a weed trimmer. He advised he did and I asked him to bring it when we met the next day.

I arrived ahead of the time we had set and rode through the property looking for the best place to utilize the deer. You can't just set a decoy up anywhere. There are several things to consider when deciding where to use the decoy with the main consideration being safety. Fortunately, Shocco had plenty of property that would work. I found what I thought would be a good spot, but as I had feared it was a little too thick, hence the weed trimmer request. You would be surprised how many times I have had a road hunter roll right past the decoy without ever seeing it. Let me contrast that with the number of times I have had someone claim they had seen my decoy whenever it was nowhere near where they said. That happened a lot and it no doubt saved the lives of a lot of deer!

I went back to the conference center maintenance area and found Greg waiting on me. I explained I had located what I thought could be transformed into a good spot but it was going to take a significant amount of brush cutting. The drawback of this was you didn't want yourself or your truck to be seen in the area but sometimes it just couldn't be helped. We drove to the site and hopped out and began clearing the area. The site I had selected was fifty-one yards off of the road on a slight grade that turned up behind the deer, providing a safe backdrop. I advised Greg we needed to make it pretty clean. He began weed trimming and I was cutting larger saplings with my saw. After we had it fairly clean I asked Greg to cut a little more. I told him our suspect had never seen the turkey we had used earlier and I felt this was going to have to be very obvious. In a few minutes we had a wildlife opening where a grown-up field had been. I told him I thought it would work and we got out of the area.

A couple of days later, Lt. Fincher, Sgt. Bassett, CEO Gilliland, and I were back on the property. The lieutenant carried me to the site and I took the decoy and set it up in our opening. He commented it sure was out in the open and I said I thought that was what we needed. He and Greg moved back to a hiding spot up the road where he could hopefully intercept anyone heading that way. I moved to a hiding spot across the road and made sure everything was working correctly. Sgt. Bassett was down the road in case the violator was headed in that direction. You never wanted to get in a chase and having units on each end helped to minimize that. With everything in place, our vigil began.

I had been set up for about an hour with the occasional car coming through when our suspect slowly passed my vantage point in his white Chevrolet SUV. I noted there was no one else in the vehicle. If he had spotted the decoy, he had not given any indication of it. When he had not come back in a couple of minutes I knew he once again had failed to see the deer. I sat and wondered how many deer he was actually shooting as poor as he was at spotting them. Of course, I knew it wouldn't take but one shot from him for a tragedy to occur.

Approximately twenty minutes later, Joe came back by my position headed in the opposite direction. Once again, he gave no indication he had seen the deer. Normally, even your better road hunters will at least let off the gas or at least turn around in the seat looking. Nothing! I was totally frustrated. The deer was so wide open it looked like it was standing in a parking lot and this "road hunter" breezed right on by it. Oh yeah, he's a big-time road hunter all right. I picked up the radio and told the others he had once again passed by without seeing a thing. Nobody said anything. Working the decoy can be tremendously exciting or extremely boring!

Approximately one minute later, I saw the white SUV coming back toward my location and moving very slowly. I quickly keyed the mic and said, "He's coming back." When he was directly in front of me he stopped his vehicle in the public road. The deer was on his passenger side. I was about twenty yards from the vehicle in the edge of the woods. Unfortunately, as he turned and looked at the deer, his body was blocking me from being able to see exactly what he was doing. However, seconds later I heard a gunshot! I called the other units and told them he had shot and to come to my location.

As I began moving toward the truck he fired again and again. When I got to where I could see, I could tell he was shooting from the driver's seat through the passenger-side window with a handgun. He fired again. I was approaching the truck and yelling for him to stop shooting and to put his gun down. He fired again.

For an officer approaching the suspect this is a more dangerous situation than approaching someone with a long gun in that the handgun can be easily turned and pointed toward the officer. Therefore, I stayed slightly behind him with my pistol in hand yelling loud verbal commands for him to put the gun down. He had yet to acknowledge my presence. His vehicle began to slowly roll forward while I continued to give loud verbal commands. CEO Bassett arrived and pulled in behind the vehicle with his blue lights activated and the man pulled the vehicle to the side of the road.

He turned and saw me and rolled his window down. I told him to put his hands up. Officer Gilliland and Lt. Fincher arrived and pulled in front of his truck. I instructed Mr. Joe to put his hands out the window and he complied. Lt. Fincher went to the passenger side of the vehicle and removed a loaded 12-gauge shotgun and a .38 Special handgun from the vehicle. Mr. Joe had fired all the shells from the handgun at the deer decoy.

I opened the driver's door of the vehicle and told him to step out. I told him to put his hands on the side of the truck and I patted him down for any other weapons. I advised him of his rights and he stated he understood. I asked, "What is going on?" His answer was priceless. He replied, "I haven't shot my pistol in a long time and thought I would shoot it." It was all I could do not to laugh out loud! I asked if the deer standing in the opening helped him make the decision to shoot his pistol and he grinned and said, "It might have." I advised him he was under arrest. We made a quick search of the area around his seat and allowed Mr. Joe, who is seventy-six years old, to sit back down in the seat.

He gave a statement saying he saw the deer and turned around and came back to shoot it. He admitted he had shot at it with his pistol and he knew it was illegal to shoot from his vehicle. When asked if he had a permit to hunt on the property he stated he did not. I asked if he knew who owned the property and he said he did not. When asked if he knew the deer season was not open, he said he thought it had opened on October 15. I explained to him the archery season opened then but the gun season would not be open for another three weeks. I asked if he had a bow and arrow and he said he did not. He then said, unsolicited, that he knew he wasn't supposed to shoot from the road.

Mr. Joe was arrested for hunting from the public road, hunting without a permit, hunting in closed season, and hunting by the aid of a vehicle. He was given a trial date for district court in Talladega.

Almost three months later, Mr. Joe appeared in Talladega district court before Judge Jeb Fannin. He pled guilty to hunting from the road, from the vehicle, and in closed season. He pled not guilty to hunting without a permit. In his defense, he stated, "There was not a Private Property or No Trespassing sign anywhere on that road!" He stated that he drove that road every day and there definitely were not any signs on it. The ADA asked him if he owned the land and he said he did not. He asked if he knew who did own the land and he said he did not. Lo and behold he was found guilty on that charge as well! The judge assessed the minimum fine in each case and waived the costs in each case. He gave him 180 days to pay the fines, which totaled $2,450.

Like many, Mr. Joe saw no problem shooting from the road and didn't understand what the deal was. Also, he believed if there weren't any posted signs then the land was open to anyone. That may have been widely accepted seventy years ago when there were much fewer folks and hunters weren't paying ten dollars or more an acre to lease property to hunt on.

At the conclusion of the court case, I wondered whether or not Mr. Joe would pay his fine. I felt certain since he had six months to get it paid, he would probably wait six months before he started paying.

A few months later, Lt. Fincher contacted me and said we would not have to worry about Mr. Joe hunting from the road anymore in that he had gone on into wherever old road hunters go when they pass away. At seventy-six years old, Joe wasn't the oldest person I had ever arrested. However, he was pretty hardcore. He had done it all of his life and evidently didn't see any reason to quit.

Heavy Flow of Info!

WHILE SOME FOLKS MAY HAVE a lot of info, it may or may not be helpful. I once received a complaint of night hunting from Tallapoosa County and it came with a phone number for the complainant. I called the number and received an earful. I identified myself as the game warden and that was about all I got out before the barrage started. The lady on the other end of the line, Mrs. McDonald, began spitting out info rapid fire.

She told me she and her husband, who was ninety-four years old, had lived in the area all of their life. Someone was shooting at night near her home. Well it was actually from the yard of the church, which was approximately one hundred yards from their house. It was actually closer to her neighbor's house. Which was about sixty yards from her house. He lives there alone. He was married but his wife left him. He does have someone else stay there from time to time but there hasn't been anyone else there lately. He probably had a better view of things than she did but he probably wouldn't tell me anything.

All of that was in one run-on nonstop sentence during which the woman did not take a breath! When she did finally pause for a breath, I wasn't sure how long it would be before I got another chance to ask a question so I quickly asked if she had any idea who it was. The barrage of info began again.

While she wasn't positive she had a good idea that it was that

Bradford boy that lived just down the road a piece over there off of Boone Road in a little white house, not the one with the white fence, but the one with an old Dodge car up on blocks and a shed on the north side of the house. She went to explain that boy had always been trouble. Back several years ago she was on her way to work and that boy was out in the road and wouldn't let her get by and just about made her late for work at the sewing plant and if you was late they would dock your pay and she had never been late and wasn't going to be late. She was so upset she told her boss man that if that boy was in the road the next day she was going to run over him and kill him. Her boss man, Mr. Johnson, tried to calm her down but she was pretty worked up. Mr. Johnson had a friend that worked with the sheriff's office and he called him and he came to the factory and talked to her. His name was Deputy Kilgore and he told her she didn't need to run over and kill that boy and she told him that she couldn't afford to be late for work and have her pay docked and she was going to run over him if he was in the road again.

At this point she took another pause to catch her breath. Although this whole story didn't necessarily have anything to do with someone shooting at night, I had heard so much I really wanted to hear the rest of it. After taking a deep breath she continued. She said Mr. Kilgore told her he was going to go and have a talk with that boy and he didn't think he would be back out in the road after he got through talking to him. Evidently whatever he said to him did the trick because she did not see him back in the road again! Whew! I had to take a big breath and I was only listening!

While I thought we might now get back to the night hunting complaint, I was mistaken. I got a good location on the church and told her I would get by and look at it and see if I could find a place to work it from. Since the location was close to the Randolph

County line, I called Sgt. Thomas Traylor and told him about Chatty Cathy and her complaint. He replied he knew some people like that. He said she only leaves home to go to church and the beauty shop yet she can tell you everything that's going on in the community. I told him he must have already met her!

I looked the place over and had a hard time figuring out where anyone would be shining and shooting near her house, which was an overgrown clear-cut area that you would be hard-pressed to see in to. However, I did find an area close by that looked promising. The first night I worked the area I heard a shot off in the distance and also had a neighbor—not the one who now lived alone except on occasion—pull in on me where I was hiding. I had just backed into a hiding spot in a clear-cut area when I saw the lights of a vehicle come on at a nearby residence. When I saw him pull out from the residence I had slipped out of my truck. This would not be the first time that I had caught a complainant's neighbor. As I watched from the rear of my truck, the vehicle came straight to my truck. He stopped short and rolled his window down and shouted, "I'm sorry, I didn't know who it was." I stepped out and told him that was okay. I asked if he had been having trouble with someone in the clear-cut and he said the landowner had asked him to keep an eye on it and he had seen my lights when I had pulled in. While that didn't necessarily answer my question, I did not see any need to engage him any further. He returned to his house and I began my long, cold visual. I did hear a shot off in the distance. I later contacted the former Tallapoosa County CEO Jeff Brown and told him where I had heard the shot and he advised it would be either Johnny Looney or Keith Downs. He explained he had caught both of them night hunting in the area previously. He said if I would turn left onto Simpson Road I would go through a bottom and cross over a small creek. I would then be going uphill and about a hundred yards on the left there was a dim road I could back up in and watch the bottom area. That kind of information was invaluable to an officer who wasn't familiar with an area. He went on to say that if I needed any more info on the area I could contact Mrs. McDonald and she could fill me in on things. I told him she was the reason I was there. He laughed and I once again realized some things just don't change!

While some folks could try your patience and you often had to listen to a lot of superfluous fluff, without receiving some info from the public, a conservation officer had a tough way to go!

Location, Location, Location

I FEEL CERTAIN MOST PEOPLE HAVE HEARD someone when speaking of real estate use the phrase *location, location, location*. That phrase indicates that identical homes can increase or decrease in value due to where they are located. Some refer to that as the number-one rule in real estate. Interestingly, that's not the only place the saying comes into play.

Let's suffice it to say choosing to shoot a deer at night is always a bad choice. That being said, some situations are worse than others. When you add one bad choice on top of another you shouldn't be surprised when things go incredibly bad!

Around 10:00 p.m. one cool early October night a homeowner observed a slow-moving pickup truck driving down the road in front of his home in Talladega County. He noticed there was an individual standing in the back of the pickup and pointing a compound bow toward his house. He came out of his door and observed an individual on the ground beside his driveway. He shined his flashlight on the subject who he described as a white male in his early twenties approximately six feet tall and around two hundred pounds. The individual immediately ran back to the truck, which was being driven by another individual, and began trying to open the passenger-side door. He was yelling, "Freddie, we gotta go. Go! Go! Go!" The man jumped in the passenger side of the vehicle and the driver sped off. The homeowner was within six feet of the truck and described it as a gray GMC pickup with large tires and loud exhaust. He also recorded the tag number.

The next morning at 7:30 the landowner went to where he had seen the man and observed a dead doe deer lying in his neighbor's yard. The deer had an arrow protruding from its rear end. The homeowner removed the arrow and noted the brand and that it was a tipped with a mechanical broadhead. In addition, the landowner spotted the truck he had observed in front of his home down the street at another residence and again took down the tag number. Talk about helpful. With this type of info coming in, the investigation moved forward quickly. You may have guessed by this time this wasn't your run-of-the-mill landowner. It was actually the investigator for the county district attorney!

We picked up the investigation and soon we had the name of the owner of the vehicle, Jimmy Staggs. A little further investigation revealed another very good suspect, Brody Sims. With two names to work with we began determining how to find the two young men and hopefully soon make their acquaintance. We felt that matching the arrow found at the scene with those possessed by Mr. Staggs would be significant. Therefore, we obtained a search warrant for Mr. Staggs's home and vehicle.

A few days later, I met with CEO Greg Gilliland and Sgt. Jason Bassett in Lincoln. As we were headed to Mr. Staggs's home, we came up behind him on the road. I felt this was ideal. In my experience you will end up with a better outcome if you don't conduct your interview at the suspect's home.

Sgt. Bassett pulled the truck over. I identified myself to Mr. Staggs as a conservation officer and member of the DCNR Special Task Force. I advised him we were investigating an incident and needed to ask him some questions. I advised him of his rights and had him read and sign a waiver. I asked if he had an idea why we were talking to him and he indicated he did. I was watching closely as he bit his lip and could tell he was very uncomfortable. Interviewing someone is very much an art and proper timing has a lot to do with it. In this situation, I decided I would try something a little out of the norm. I looked at the young man and asked him, "Do you want to tell me what happened or do you want me to tell you?" This had the effect I wanted. I could tell he was now in a quandary and wasn't sure how to answer. My intent was to get him off of whatever he had been thinking he would say. Obviously, it had worked because he wasn't saying anything. He was just looking at me with a fairly pitiful look. The young man finally said, "You tell me."

I began by saying I felt like he had made some bad decisions and while that didn't mean he was a bad person, decisions have consequences. I told him he had shot a deer with an arrow while he was standing in the bed of his truck with his friend Brody driving. I could literally see him sagging down with every detail I provided. In addition to sagging, he was slowly nodding his head in agreement with all I was saying. I added that someone had seen him and identified him and his truck. I asked if that sounded about right and he nodded his head in the affirmative. I told him I would need to get a statement from him and he again nodded his head yes.

He gave a full statement in which he admitted he had been the man in the back of the truck driven by Brody Sims and he had shot at a deer with his bow on property for which he did not have permission to hunt from his vehicle that was sitting in the public road. He stated he had exited the truck with a light to look for the deer when someone approached him. He ran to the truck shouting for the driver to open the door. He jumped in and they sped away.

I asked if he had his bow and arrows with him and he said he did. I asked if we could look at them and he removed them from the truck and gave them to us. The arrows and broadheads were a perfect match to the arrow retrieved from the deer on the scene. We completed his statement and advised him we would be in touch with him. I told him we appreciated his cooperation. I asked if he had a phone number for Mr. Sims and he provided it to us.

We contacted Mr. Sims and set up a meeting with him. I advised him of his rights and he signed a waiver. He was very straightforward and acknowledged everything that had taken place. He also gave a statement which was very closely aligned with Mr. Staggs's statement. He admitted he had driven the truck and was a willing participant in the illegal hunting. He stated he knew he had made a major mistake and he knew there would be repercussions. However, he explained hunting was his life and he desperately did not want to lose his hunting privileges. I advised him that wasn't up to us and we were not sure what would happen in that regard.

Based on our investigation, witness statement, physical evidence, and confessions from both suspects we obtained warrants for hunting at night, hunting from a public road, hunting by aid of a vehicle, and hunting without a permit. In addition, they received warnings for hunting within one hundred yards of a dwelling, hunting in closed season, and hunting without a license. The pair appeared in district court where they pled guilty to all charges and paid heavy fines.

If you are old enough to remember Paul Harvey, then you will understand when I say here's the rest of the story. You may wonder why this was entitled "Location, Location, Location." As I mentioned the deer was shot in the yard of the district attorney's investigator. Not a wise move. What I did not have to use in the investigation due to getting confessions was the fact that the investigator's Ring doorbell had caught all of the violations on camera. You could see the man standing in the bed of the truck. You could hear the driver telling the hunter to shoot the deer. You

171

could hear the bow go off and could even hear the deer bleat after being shot! The entire case was all caught on video. I'm sure you will agree that was a bad location to commit such an offense. But that's not all!

While the deer was shot in the investigator's yard that was not where it expired. Although mortally wounded, the large doe was able to make her way off of the investigator's property and onto the neighbor's property. The neighbor was the Talladega County circuit judge!

Just so you know the subjects were treated fairly, they pled guilty so there was not a trial where the investigator/landowner could have been called to testify. The subjects were given minimum fines by the district judge and the circuit judge was not involved.

This was almost as bad as when the drunk night hunters shot the game warden's hog in the pen next to his house!! Some folks sure make some bad choices!!

Extreme
Hunter Harassment

I MUST ADMIT I NORMALLY don't get many hunting complaints in August. That can likely be attributed to there being no major hunting seasons open and the temperature is normally in the low to midnineties! That being said I was a little surprised when I was contacted by a hunter who reported some problems with his hunting property in the Richville community of Coosa County. He stated he had recently set up a feeder and a shooting house on the property where he had permission to hunt and when he had returned to the property he found his feeder had been disabled and his salt block had been placed inside his shooting house, which had also been moved. He said Mr. Jim Dabbs, who lives in a house on the property, told him he had moved the items because he felt they were too close to his house. I immediately realized these details, if true, would constitute a violation of our hunter harassment law. I advised the hunter I would open an investigation and would be back with him. I told to inform me if anything else took place. Little did I know how extensive this situation would be.

Interestingly our "interference with persons legally hunting or fishing" law was put in place to combat hunt protesters who were prevalent at some locations in the country at that time.

These folks would often harass legal hunters when they were in the field, which often led to serious confrontations. Fortunately, I never used the law in that type situation. However, I have used it a few times in cases such as this one.

One of the elements of the law that must be satisfied before it can be enforced is that the person being harassed is hunting or fishing legally. Therefore, I needed to verify the fellow making the report did in fact have permission to hunt on the property. The fact that the alleged suspect actually lived on the property was also an interesting twist.

I checked our county tax records and determined who actually owned the property. I contacted the landowner, who lived out of state, to ascertain who had what authority on the property. He told me the complainant had the hunting privileges on the property and the fellow living on the property had been allowed to stay in the house but did not have permission to be on the property except for the yard of the house. Obviously, there were some problems with that setup.

On the third of September I received another call from the hunter stating someone had driven through his recently planted green fields damaging them. In an effort to stop the problem before it got any worse I went to meet with the suspect. I introduced myself and advised him I was there to discuss the hunting on the property. Before I said anything else or asked any questions, he began telling me about his encounter with the hunter. He said the young man had come into his yard and gotten irate with him because he had moved his shooting house and stuff. He went on to say he had moved it because it was too close to his house. I mentally made note of his spontaneous exclamation, which told me he was already in violation of the law.

I told him the hunter had contacted me and that was why I was there. I explained there was a law against harassing hunters and what he had done was in violation of that law. He replied, "Yeah, but I live here." I told him it was my understanding he had no permission to be on any of the property except for the house and yard. He immediately asked who had said that and I told him the landowner had told me that. He got a very surprised look on his face and said, "You talked to the landowner?" I told him I had and I again told him I was advised he had no authority over the property and no permission to be anywhere on the property other than at the house. At that point, another man, who said his name was Hector, asked could they not ride four-wheelers on the property and I told him the landowner had said no one, besides the hunter, had permission to be anywhere but at the house. He replied he was glad he had asked.

The resident said he had ridden over to see if the shooting house and feeder had been put back and it had. The other fellow commented the corn wasn't ten yards from the shooting house. I told him that wasn't illegal. I reiterated to the pair that they were not to be on the property other than the yard of the house. Mr. Dabbs again stated the hunter had come into the yard and caused a scene and there was no reason for him to come back in the yard. I told him I was there to prevent a confrontation between them and to make sure they understood they could not harass the hunter and messing with his hunting property constituted harassing him. Mr. Dabbs again said the young man had harassed him when he came in his yard and I told him he should not do that again. I told him if there was any more harassment from either side, I would be handling it. He stated he understood, and I left.

The next morning, my phone blew up with pictures from the hunter. Several of them showed where four-wheelers had driven through his food plot. In addition, there was a rope fashioned into a hangman's noose hanging out of the window of his shooting house. I felt it was obvious my talk with Mr. Dabbs had fallen on deaf ears. I was documenting everything and building a solid harassment case.

About a month later the gun deer season opened. The hunter contacted me and stated someone had mowed strips through the deer bedding area on the property. Unfortunately, although I felt certain Mr. Dabbs was the one causing all of the problems, thinking it and proving it in court are two different things. While he admitted moving the shooting house, that was before the season and I felt things would be much stronger if we could document some activities during the gun deer season.

Five days later near dark the hunter contacted me and reported Mr. Dabbs had been running the leaf blower since about four in the afternoon. He said due to the noise, he and his young daughter had left the woods. As he drove down the county road, he observed Mr. Dabbs using the leaf blower to blow pine needles out of the public road. The hunter pulled his truck up beside Mr. Dabbs, who asked, "Can I help you?" The hunter replied, "Yes," and then took a picture of the man holding the leaf blower in the public road. I asked him to send me the picture and told him I felt we had enough and I would talk with the district attorney (DA) about obtaining warrants.

The next day Mr. Dabbs pulled the same stunt with the leaf blower. He was two hundred yards from his house. The following day "someone" had placed a large pile of pine needles in the area where the hunter had been parking his truck. To avoid confrontation, he had been parking his truck approximately three hundred yards from the dwelling on the property. When he entered the hunting area he found "someone" had been mowing strips through the hunting area again.

"Interference with persons legally hunting or fishing" is very clear when it says, "No person shall willfully and knowingly prevent, obstruct, impede, disturb, or interfere with, or attempt to prevent, obstruct, impede, disturb, or interfere with any person in legally hunting or fishing pursuant to the rules and regulations of the Department of Conservation and Natural Resources and the law of the State of Alabama." The hunter harassment law is interesting in that it goes into great detail about what activities are prohibited. It plainly states that you cannot create a visual, aural, olfactory, or physical stimulus intended to affect the natural behavior of the wild animal being hunted or fish for the purpose of fishing. Furthermore, it says you cannot affect the condition or location of personal property intended for use in the hunting or fishing.

I felt Mr. Dabbs had violated the law in just about every way he could. I spoke with DA Joe Ficquette and updated him on the latest happenings. He advised me to obtain a warrant and get that guy in front of the judge. I immediately went and obtained a warrant for Mr. Dabbs for hunter harassment.

I obtained the warrant and immediately went to Mr. Dabbs's house. However, I was unable to get anyone to the door. Subsequent attempts were also unsuccessful. I contacted my longtime friend, Coosa SO Corporal Mike Rudd and advised him I had a warrant for Mr. Dabbs and to keep a lookout for him. A few days later Mike called and told me there were multiple vehicles at the residence. I told him I would be there momentarily.

We knocked on the door and the walls of the house. We called out for Mr. Dabbs to come out and got no response. We stayed there for probably twenty-five minutes and left. A couple of days later I drove by the residence and spotted Mr. Dabbs in the yard. I pulled in the drive and exited my truck and he walked over to me. I identified myself and read him the Miranda warning. He stated he understood. I asked if he remembered me talking with him earlier and he said he did and he had not been bothering anyone. I asked if he had been mowing strips in the woods and he said he had been mowing the walking trails where they walk in the woods. I asked if he remembered me telling him he was not to be in the woods according to the landowner and he said he did. I told him I had a warrant for his arrest for interfering with someone legally hunting and he was under arrest. He stated he hated it but he understood I was just doing my job. I filled out a bond and allowed him to sign it. I advised him of the court date and told him he needed to be there. He advised he understood.

I contacted the hunter and advised him Mr. Dabbs had been arrested and told him he should not initiate any contact with him. I advised him of the court date and told him I would have him subpoenaed if that was necessary for him. He said he would definitely be there.

The court date rolled around and the complainant was there but the defendant was not. The judge called the docket and when Mr. Dabbs was not present he issued a failure-to-appear warrant for him. I advised the complainant he was free to go and we would let him know when he needed to come back. After he had left, you guessed it, Mr. Dabbs showed up. I called the complainant and asked if he could come back and he said he would.

The judge called the case and Mr. Dabbs asked that an attorney be appointed for his case. The judge granted the request and the lawyer immediately asked that the case be continued until the next month. The judge granted that request and I had to tell the hunter he had come to court twice today for nothing.

On the day prior to court, the attorney, a young girl who I had known since she was a child, contacted me and stated her client was having a medical problem and she wasn't sure whether he would be in court or not. She continued saying the complainant would not need to appear as they planned to plead guilty. With some folks this would have been problematic. If the witness isn't there and they decide to plead not guilty you could easily lose the case. I was not worried about that with this attorney. I felt certain I could testify to enough of the case to convict the defendant if necessary. I called the complainant and told him he would not need to come as Mr. Dabbs was supposed to plead guilty.

The next day I met with the attorney and she asked what we were looking for as far as a sentence was concerned. I told her we wanted a fine and some probation time with a no-contact order. She said the range was $0–$500 and asked if $250 and cost and twelve months of unsupervised probation with a no-contact order would be sufficient. I told her that sounded good to me. The judge called for settled cases and we stepped forward and explained the agreement to him. He accepted it and we were finished.

I kept an eye on the area and failed to see anyone at the house. I soon learned Mr. Dabbs had vacated the premises and moved on to places unknown! Not long after this I was contacted by a friend of mine who asked for the details of the case. I gave him a brief synopsis. He informed me he had heard from a local guy on how badly I had mistreated Mr. Dabbs and how he had not done anything wrong. I told him I had documented at least eight incidents where the man had harassed the hunter who was hunting legally. I knew the man who said the defendant had been done wrong and I told my friend that Mr. Dabbs was looking for a place to stay and maybe he could move next to that guy! That type of armchair quarterbacking was quite common. While it was aggravating, I was confident the defendant was as guilty as one could get and deserved all that he got.

Would You Like to Start Over?

As I have written many times, there is no substitute for receiving information from the public. While you can work on your own and come up with some cases, receiving information helps an officer cut down their search area significantly. Therefore, when we receive information we do our best to respond to it.

One winter morning I received a call from Conservation Enforcement Officer Jinks Altiere concerning shooting from the road in the Windemere housing development at Lake Martin in Tallapoosa County. Windemere is a high-end housing area on the largest man-made lake in the country. The area is loaded with million-dollar homes and a dense population of white-tailed deer which makes for a difficult combination.

The complainant advised upon hearing a shot close by, he jumped in his truck and went to the location. He observed a white male loading a deer in the bed of his truck. He said the man left at a high rate of speed but not before he was able to get some video. We told him we would come to his home and view the video as soon as possible.

I got up with Jinks and we headed over. We met our complainant and he again explained he had heard the really loud shot and had immediately gone to the area. There he observed a young white male who was pulling a white-tailed buck into the bed of his truck. He began videoing and fortunately got both a picture of the man and the license plate number of the truck. We took a statement from him and told him we would be in touch.

I ran the tag number and it came back to someone I was familiar with. It just so happened that the young man had gone to school with my son. I immediately called Lt. Jerry Fincher and advised him of what we had and asked if he could go to the young man's address in hopes he would find a deer there. Jerry went to the residence and did in fact find a deer there; however, the young man's father claimed he had killed the deer. He also advised the officer that his son had moved to another county. Jerry obtained the son's telephone number and gave him a call. He advised him we needed to talk with him and set up a meeting for the next day. Learning that, I immediately began pulling together a background on the young man and developing a series of questions for his interview.

As it turned out Jinks was unable to accompany me to the interview; however, Lt. Fincher said he would meet me there. In my way of thinking one of the most important things you can do when preparing for an interview is to try to anticipate what the suspect will use as a defense and do your best to figure out how to negate it. In this situation, I felt like I held the upper hand having the picture of him holding a deer in the back of his truck. However, the picture wasn't really clear and I hoped he would come clean without me having to show it to him.

The suspect arrived at the church parking lot driving a truck that closely resembled the one in the picture. After introductions, I advised him I wanted to ask him some questions and for his protection I wanted to advise him of his rights. I read him the Miranda warning and he stated he understood. He was very calm.

I began with some basic questions. We verified the truck he was driving was in fact his and no one else drove it regularly. I asked if he had been driving it in Tallapoosa County on the previous day. He advised he had been and he had gone to some land he hunted to put out some feed. I asked whose land he hunted on and he gave me the landowner's name and said the man owned ten acres there. I commented that wasn't a lot of land to hunt and he advised he only hunted with a bow and there were a lot of deer in the area. I asked if he had hunted there yesterday and he replied he had not. I asked if he owned a rifle and he said he did. I asked if he had it with him yesterday and he said he did not. I asked if he owned a handgun and he said he did own a 9 mm and he had it with him.

The fellow was answering all of my questions without hesitation and he was extremely smooth. Most people being questioned in that manner were normally not at ease, but this fellow wasn't anxious at all. He was so smooth I was beginning to wonder whether or not he was the right guy. I asked the lieutenant if he had any questions. He asked a question and I went to my truck and got the folder that had the picture of the man in the back of the truck. I looked at the photo and then looked at the truck. I was wondering if the fuzzy picture may not have been his truck. However, an old investigator once told me when you are doing an investigation, there is no such thing as coincidence. I was thinking it could not be coincidence that he was in the area but had not done the shooting. I looked at the picture again and noticed the truck had an enlarged exhaust pipe that hid part of the rear tire. I moved back around behind the truck and realized it was a match.

Feeling confident, I asked the suspect how he would respond if I told him I had a photo of him loading a deer into his truck in Windemere yesterday. I could tell that possibility shook his confidence, but he stayed the course and didn't admit to anything.

I removed the picture of him standing in the bed of his truck with the deer from the folder and asked, "Does this look like you?" He hung his head. With his confidence now gone, Lt. Fincher asked, "Would you like to start over?" He said he would. He apologized for lying to us but said he did not know how much the man had seen and he wasn't going to confess to anything if the man didn't have any proof.

He went on to say he had seen a very large buck in the area and that was why he had the rifle in the truck. He drove down the road and saw a spike buck standing alongside the road. As he looked at it, he saw a doe and a buck bedded down in the woods. He pulled his truck off the edge of the road and shot the bedded buck through his passenger side window with his .243 Browning BAR rifle. He said it never moved. He got out of the truck and dragged the deer up to it. As he was loading it into his truck, a small truck pulled up behind him. He got into his truck and went to the main road and headed toward Tuscaloosa. He said he carried the deer to a friend's house in Coosa County where he cleaned it. He admitted he did not report the harvest and did not have a permit to hunt where he shot the deer. We took a statement and told him we appreciated him coming clean and we would be in touch.

I obtained warrants for hunting without a permit and hunting from a public road. I decided to issue warnings for hunting by the aid of a vehicle and failure to complete a harvest record. The subject appeared in Tallapoosa District Court and pled guilty to the charges and paid the fines and court costs that day. I'm sure you've heard the old adage a picture is worth a thousand words. In this case it was worth $2,000!

Whose Property
Were You Shining?

TOWARD THE END OF MY CAREER, I put together some training for non-conservation law enforcement officers. This was done out of necessity. While I always appreciated assistance from other law enforcement, unfortunately they knew very little about our laws and regulations and how they were enforced. While they were trying to help they often messed things up. One incident that quickly comes to mind was the time I had responded to a night hunting complaint and put the suspect vehicle information out over the radio. While I was still on the scene, a trooper radioed he had stopped a vehicle matching the description. I hurried to his location. Unfortunately, prior to my arrival, the trooper had removed the gun from the vehicle and sniffed it and told the two teenagers it had not been shot. Because the victim, whose yard they shot in, had given me very detailed information, I knew these were in fact the culprits. I obtained warrants for them. When they appeared in court, the first thing their attorney said to me was the trooper had stated their gun had not been shot. I told him the trooper wasn't a firearms expert. See "That Didn't Happen" in my previous book, *He's Still Shooting*.

The training I put together included that story and several others. I also told the officers not to fall into some of the fallacies that a lot of people believed such as all night hunters drove pickup trucks, shot only rifles, and were all men. I taught the class multiple times in various counties. I ended it by advising the officers if they felt they had something we needed to assist them on to call us any time day or night.

One night at approximately 10:18 p.m. I received a call from Coosa County Deputy Travis Ward who informed me he had stopped a white Ford Ranger pickup on Coosa County Road 78 after observing the driver, Gerald Gee, shining a spotlight from the driver's side window. I asked if Mr. Gee possessed a firearm and was informed he in fact had three firearms in the vehicle. I informed the deputy I would be en route.

I arrived on the scene and asked the deputy what he had observed. He stated as he and Reserve Deputy Shane Payton came up behind the truck they observed the driver as he shined a spotlight out of the driver-side window. The light illuminated the roadside and wood line for a few seconds before it was extinguished.

The deputy stated he immediately activated his blue lights, but Mr. Gee continued down the road for a short distance before coming to a stop. When Deputy Ward approached the driver's window, he observed Mr. Gee was still holding the spotlight in his hand. The deputy informed him he wasn't supposed to shine a light out the window and the man replied, "Didn't you see that deer back there?" Deputy Ward told Mr. Gee it was illegal to spotlight deer and he replied he did not know that. The officer saw the rifle which was in the extended cab section of the vehicle. He asked if there were any other weapons and Mr. Gee stated he had a derringer in his pocket and a pistol in the glove box.

I moved to Mr. Gee and advised Mr. Gee of his rights via the Miranda warning. I asked what was going on and he stated he and his girlfriend had been to the casino in Wetumpka and were on their way home. I asked about him shining the light out the window and he stated he did not shine the light out the window. He explained he had remembered he had not left a light on at his home and he would need the light to see how to get in, so he reached and got it out of the extended cab section of the truck. He said he had accidently turned the light on, and it shined on his window. I asked how far it was to his house and he replied it was about a mile.

I went back to the deputy and asked whether Mr. Gee's window was down, and he said he saw the light out the window and shining on the property off the side of the road. I separately spoke with the reserve officer and asked him to tell me what he had observed. He said they saw Mr. Gee shine the spotlight out the window into a low area off the side of the road and into the wood line.

I went to Mr. Gee's truck and observed a .22-caliber semiautomatic rifle, in plain view, in the extended part of the cab of the truck. I photographed the gun in the truck. I noticed the safety was off on the firearm. I asked Mr. Gee if the gun was loaded, and he said he was not sure. I checked the gun and found it was loaded. I engaged the safety and returned the gun to where it had been.

I again spoke with Mr. Gee and explained shining the light from the truck at night in an area where deer are known to frequent combined with having the rifle fulfilled all the elements of a night hunting case. He replied he did not even have a hunting license. He said he had the rifle in case he saw a coyote. I advised him his story and the deputy's story did not match very well. I called the deputy over and told him Mr. Gee had said he had inadvertently activated the light while removing it from behind the seat but had not shined it out of the window. The deputy asked Mr. Gee what he had said to him when he had walked up to the window. When he did not respond the deputy said, "You asked him if I had seen the deer back there?" At this point, Mr. Gee said, "It [the deer] ran across the road right in front of us." I felt that pretty well wrapped things up. I thanked Deputy Ward and told him I would be finished with Mr. Gee shortly.

I made sure I had all the information needed to obtain warrants for the man. I did not plan to arrest his girlfriend as she was a passenger and wasn't in control of anything. I had one more question for Mr. Gee but I knew I needed to ask the question in a casual manner. I told Mr. Gee I felt I had all the info I needed and that I would be back in touch with him. As he turned and began walking toward his truck, I called to him and asked, "Whose property were you shining?" and without hesitation he replied, "It was Johnny Smith's property." I asked if he had a permit from Mr. Smith and he replied he did not. That was the answer I was looking for.

Based on the evidence at hand, primarily the statements from the deputies, I felt the suspect fulfilled all the elements of the crimes of hunting at night, hunting from the public road, hunting from the aid of a vehicle, and hunting without a permit. Therefore, I obtained warrants for three of the charges. I did not acquire a warrant for hunting without a permit.

A few days later I went to Mr. Gee's residence and served the warrants. Mr. Gee and his girlfriend were argumentative and continued stating that was not what they were doing. I advised them that was why we had court and they could plead their case there.

The next month we were in court and I was advised Mr. Gee had been appointed an attorney. Partway through court I was approached by a young girl probably in her midtwenties who asked if I was the arresting officer in the Gee cases. I advised her I was. She explained she had never handled a hunting case and was not familiar with the game laws. I asked if she would like for me to explain to her what had occurred and she said she would appreciate it. I laid out the case for her and described how Mr. Gee had fulfilled all the elements of the cases. I explained I had statements from the deputies and body cam footage. She asked if there was any way I could work with her on it and I told her if he wanted to plead guilty to the cases we could possibly remit some of the fines and costs if the judge wanted to. She thanked me and we both returned to the courtroom. The judge called the man's name and the attorney approached the bench. The judge asked if she had been able to work anything out and she advised we would need to go to trial. I must admit my first thought was so much for working something out. She asked if the cases could be continued and the judge granted the continuance. Don't get me started on continued cases! I gathered my stuff and left the courtroom.

During the next month, I went back over the evidence and made sure I was well prepared in the event we did go to trial. At court the attorney again asked to speak with me outside the courtroom. This time her demeanor was somewhat different. She explained she had read the report and watched the video and she wanted to know how I could work with her on the cases. My response was I was ready to work with her last month but now I was ready to go to trial. Her mouth fell open and she said, "You mean you won't work with me?" I replied I had offered to work with her last month. I told her I felt I had been more than helpful to her last month and she then told the judge we would have to go to trial and I didn't think that sounded like cooperation. She said she had not seen the evidence at that point. I asked if she had seen it now and she said she had and I asked her how she felt now. It was obvious she wasn't sure what to say. I told her I wasn't trying to be ugly to her but this was going to have to be a two-way street.

She recomposed herself and said the fines were really high and Mr. Gee didn't have the money to pay them. I told her the fines were high for a reason and making this type of case was very difficult and the activity was very dangerous. I knew she had no experience with game and fish cases so I continued and told her I had been to houses that had been shot into by people hunting at night and had seen horses and cows shot at night. I let her know I took these types of offenses seriously and I hoped she could understand that. She was looking like a whipped puppy.

I again told her I wasn't trying to be ugly to her and I would make her the same offer as before. If he wanted to plead guilty to all three charges then I would be okay with dropping the fines and costs on the hunting from the road and hunting from the vehicle and he would have to pay the minimum fine and cost on hunting at night and he would lose his hunting privileges for three years. She replied that would still be $2,350. I replied that if we went to trial it would be $4,300! She stated she would present it to him and I told her that would be fine.

We both returned to the courtroom and she went to consult with her client. I could tell she was having a hard time selling it to him. She left him and went and spoke with another attorney from her firm. She then approached me and asked if I could cut the fine to $1,000? I told her I would not do that since the judge did not like to go below the minimum fine. It was obvious she was exasperated. She told me the man was very hard to deal with and I responded I had experienced that in my dealings with him.

The judge called for a recess to give attorneys a chance to speak with the district attorney (DA) and possibly work out cases. Luckily the DA was walking past me so I told him what we had discussed and that she had come back wanting to cut the minimum fine in half. He looked at me and said, "We aren't doing that." He said he would talk to her.

The judge returned and put court back in session. He asked if anyone had reached an agreement. Mr. Gee and his attorney approached and she told the judge we had reached an agreement. She laid it out for the judge. He added it up and told her it would be $2,350 dollars. She then told the judge her client was on a very limited income and would need time to pay. The judge looked a little uneasy and asked what she had in mind and she stated he felt he could pay $25 a month. The judge immediately said, "We aren't doing that." She again explained the man was on a very limited income. The judge tapped on his calculator and finally informed the defendant that he would allow him to pay $50 per month. Then he added that would be every month and the first payment he missed he would start serving his thirty days in jail on each charge. He asked, in a not-so-nice tone, if they both understood that and they replied they did and the case was concluded.

About three months later, I had carried my two dogs to the vet to get rabies shots and flea and tick medicine. While in the office I was talking with the vet's assistant. She said it had poured rain at her house the previous night and I told her I had had a lot of rain as well. She asked where I lived and I replied I lived in Rockford. She cocked her head to the side and said, "You're the game warden!" I could tell she wasn't happy about that. She then said, "We were not night hunting!" It was then I recognized her as the passenger in the truck in this incident. Fortunately, the vet came in and she left the room. Unfortunately, she had left the room and gone to prepare my bill. What normally had cost less than $200 that day cost me almost $400!

Fast-forward about five months. I got a call from Lt. Jerry Fincher. He explained he had received a call from a man saying he had been done wrong by someone in our department. He went on to say he had been arrested for hunting at night but the officer

190

had not handled things like he should and he wanted something done about it. Jerry asked him where this had happened and he told him it was in Coosa County. Seeing how I was the only officer working in Coosa at the time, that pretty well limited things. Jerry asked him if the officer was Joel Glover and he said it was. Although Jerry was very familiar with the case, he asked him what had been done incorrectly. Mr. Gee told him I had not arrested him on the scene but had come to his house and written him tickets about a week later and that I couldn't do that. Jerry asked him why I couldn't do that and he replied that was what he had been told. Jerry asked him what his attorney had told him and he said he had not talked to her about it. Seeing things weren't going his way, he moved on to say the fine was way too high and he couldn't afford to pay it. Jerry told him what had occurred was I had conducted an investigation and concluded he should be charged. Then I had obtained warrants for him and served them on him and allowed him to sign his bond instead of taking him to jail. He ended the conversation by saying if he wasn't happy with the outcome he needed to take that up with his attorney. Jerry said he concluded things by telling the man that if I was the one who had arrested him, he could bet it was done correctly. I appreciated his saying that. I think I trained him pretty well!

Hiding in the Barn, You Got Us, Mr. Glover

WHILE WORKING NIGHT HUNTING near Goodwater, the largest town in Coosa County, on a mid-January night, I heard the Coosa County Sheriff's Office dispatcher call a deputy and report she had received a call of night hunting on Wilson Lane in the Stewartville community. I advised her I would be en route from Goodwater.

As I raced across the county the dispatcher again called the deputy and told him a dark-colored pickup had left Wilson Lane headed toward Stewartville. The deputy responded he was on the Coleman Road and should see the truck momentarily. Within a minute Corporal Rudd radioed he was stopping the pickup. I advised him I would be on scene with him in about two minutes. I advised the other SO units to go to Wilson Lane and see if they could see anything there.

I arrived and noticed there was only one person in the truck. Corporal Rudd met me at the back of the truck and told me the driver had stated he had just left Wilson Lane and he had a high-powered rifle in the passenger seat. I identified myself and told the driver I needed to ask him some questions. I advised him of his Miranda rights and asked him to tell me where he had been. He said he had been on Wilson Lane where he was moving into a residence. I asked if he had been hunting and he said he had not. I asked to see his driver's license and found it had an out-of-town address and was expired. I asked a few other benign questions and then told him I was investigating a shots-fired call on Wilson Lane and asked if he had heard any shooting over there. He replied he had heard a shot but wasn't sure where it had come from. I asked if it had possibly come from his rifle and he assured me it had not. I asked if he would accompany me back over there and show me where he was moving to. I was a little surprised when he said he would.

I followed the driver to a trailer on a high hill overlooking Wilson Lane. We stopped and got out and I immediately spotted a cooler sitting by the door to the trailer. I asked him what was in the cooler and he replied it was deer meat. I asked where he had obtained it and he replied a friend had given it to him. Although his story was pretty shaky, I had not heard anything I could do much with. As I was telling him I appreciated his cooperation, I received a call from Deputy Logan Mitchell who advised I needed to come to their location which was at a barn on the other side of Wilson Lane. I arrived at the barn to find Deputy Mitchell, Deputy Scott, and Reserve Deputy Payton. Logan advised me dispatch had received a call that someone had seen a light in the barn and thought that was the location where they had heard the shot. The deputy said they had arrived at the barn and found a black pickup truck there. They knocked on the barn door but did not get an answer. However, they did see what appeared to be a dead deer lying inside the barn.

As we approached the barn, the door started to open. A fellow stuck his head out and immediately raised his hands and said, "I did it, I'm the one that shot." The deputies immediately grabbed the man and handcuffed him. A second man stepped out of the barn and was also handcuffed. I asked the first man to accompany me to my truck and asked the deputies to put the second subject in one of the cars.

I asked the man his name and he replied his name was Michael Winslow and he had made a bad decision and he wanted to cooperate. I asked a deputy to remove the cuffs from him. I read him the Miranda warning and had him sign a Miranda form. I asked him to tell me what had happened. He stated his friend Mark Black had picked him up at his house just up the road and he had brought his Savage 6.5 Creedmoor rifle in case they saw a deer. Mark pulled down to the barn, which was owned by Wayne Watts, Mr. Black's grandfather. The lights of the truck illuminated the field beyond the barn and they spotted a deer in the field. Mr. Winslow said he opened the door and shot the deer, which was an eight-point buck. They took the gun in the barn and went down and dragged the deer up and placed it in the barn. He said they were sitting in the barn catching their breath before they were going to begin dressing the deer and they heard a vehicle pull up. Someone came and knocked on the barn door. Knowing they had "screwed up" they did not answer the door. Eventually they heard more vehicles arriving and realized they needed to come out. He said when he heard the game warden was on the scene he knew he had to come out because we had more authority than any other officer. That wasn't necessarily the case but I didn't want to argue with the man.

Mr. Winslow stated he had not bought any hunting license. He said he had just shot the deer for the meat. I asked if he had a permit to hunt the property where the deer was shot and he said he did not. He also had not reported the harvest prior to moving the deer. I wrote out his statement and read it to him and he signed it. As I was concluding things he stated he thought I knew his father. I asked what his name was and when he told me I did immediately recognized it.

I advised Mr. Black of his rights and he stated he understood and signed a Miranda rights form. I asked him to tell me what had happened. He stated he had picked up Mr. Winslow. I asked if he knew why Mr. Winslow had brought his gun and he said in case they saw a deer they could shoot. He said he pulled down to the barn and in his headlights, they saw a buck standing in the pasture and Mr. Winslow shot it. I asked if he had shot it from the truck and he said he did. I asked what they did next and he said they put the gun in the barn. I asked if he helped drag the deer out of the field and he replied he had. He further said he was Mr. Winslow's accomplice in all of it. I wrote out his statement and he signed it.

I make it a habit to ask arrestees if they have had any prior game and fish arrests. When I asked Mr. Black if he had ever received a game and fish ticket he immediately replied, "From you!" I told him I did not recall it and he said it was on the management area and it had cost him $150.

I told both men I appreciated their honesty and I explained I would be in touch with them soon to handle the paperwork and set their court date. Both men apologized several times for what they had done. I thanked the deputies for their help and went back to where I had been working earlier.

Based on their total cooperation, I decided I would charge the two men with hunting at night and issue warnings for several other charges including hunting by the aid of a vehicle, no hunting license, and failure to report a deer harvest. I obtained the warrants and set up a time to meet with the subjects. I allowed them to sign their bonds and be on their way.

The court date rolled around and the two men were in court. The judge called Mr. Winslow up and asked if he wanted to be represented by an attorney. He told him he was guilty and did not need an attorney. The judge had him sign a waiver and then accepted his plea of guilty.

Mr. Black's case was called and the judge asked if he wanted to have an attorney appointed. Mr. Black turned and looked at me as if to ask if he needed an attorney or not. I asked if he was going to plead guilty and he said he was. Then for some reason, he turned to the judge and stated he would like to have an attorney. I wasn't sure I understood all I knew about that. He was appointed an attorney and then pled guilty. Go figure.

I requested the minimum fine and the judge agreed to that and advised the men they could go and pay the clerk. Although we had whittled it down significantly, the fine was still a hefty amount.

A final note: I had told Mr. Winslow I did know his father. I had arrested him for shooting the deer decoy. I did not mention I also knew his grandfather, who I had arrested twice for shooting the decoy, and I had dealt with his sister in a night hunting case where I arrested four men, one of which was her boyfriend. I would say I was pretty familiar with the family. As for Mr. Black, I looked up his past management area violation and found it had been nine years and hundreds of cases earlier. However, I have written several times before, when someone receives a ticket from the game warden, they never forget it.

Ticket Illegal or
Going-to-Jail Illegal?

I HAVE OFTEN STATED one of the best parts of my job was never knowing what would come along next. After retiring and coming back to work on the ADCNR Game Warden Special Task Force, I realized things had not changed a lot, with one major exception. A somewhat new duty had been added to the game warden plate and that was Range Safety Officer duties. Having officers work on shooting ranges was an opportunity to tap into some federal funding that had not been available previously. Our department decided to maximize the time CEOs spent on the ranges. This was not just an effort to receive funds. Interestingly the ranges were now a place that received a tremendous amount of activity by shooters and hunters. Some days there was standing room only at the ranges!

Although Coosa County was bordered on the east by the largest man-made lake in the country, Lake Martin, and on the west by the Coosa River, we had very few areas that offered bank fishing in the county. Therefore, the summer months allowed a good amount of time that could be spent on the shooting range at Coosa Wildlife Management Area (WMA).

Way back in 1998 our departmental leadership contacted me and said they had decided they wanted to build a shooting range on the Coosa WMA. My reply was "Why?" I went on to tell them that if people in Coosa County wanted to shoot they just stepped outside and shot. Not necessarily interested in my opinion, they instructed me to find a suitable location. They shared the needed particulars and told me to get right on it.

I soon located an area I thought would work and let them know. The hunter education coordinator came and viewed the site and gave it his blessing. Then I was told to construct the range! Fortunately, my assistant on the WMA, Ricky Porch, was a top-notch dozer operator. He went to work and the range was taking shape in short order. With the dozer work complete, it was time for us to pour the concrete slab and build the shooting benches. While we had a little experience pouring concrete, the shooting benches were new to us. Seeing how neither of us had ever laid any concrete blocks, we weren't sure what we would do. After studying the situation, we decided to set the blocks how we wanted and then pour them full of concrete. For a couple of amateur range builders, I felt it turned out pretty well. I can tell you it turned out well enough that it lasted for over twenty-five years! I will also tell you I was totally wrong when I thought the range wouldn't get much use. I'm sure there have been millions of rounds fired on the range. As I am reviewing this story, the range has been totally renovated. Hopefully it will last another twenty-five years!

Back to my story. I usually tried to check the range early in the morning. That was especially true on days when our heat index was over one hundred degrees. On one such morning I had spent some time monitoring the range and was then patrolling along a county road that normally received very little traffic. As I eased down the road my phone began to ring. I looked at it and saw the call was from the biologist aide on the Coosa WMA. Luckily, I had enough service to answer the call. Ben, the WMA aide, asked if I was anywhere close to the area and I told him I was. He proceeded to tell me about a fellow he had encountered the day before.

He advised he had come upon a suspicious man on road number 155 and he felt the fellow needed to be checked out. He explained the man had a camp set up in the middle of the road and there was something wrong about the guy. He said the fellow gave him a bad feeling and he did not know what he might be up to. He said he had told the guy it was illegal to camp where he was. He added he felt I shouldn't go in there by myself. I told him I would check it out.

I called CEO Senior Marcus Rowell and asked if he wanted to accompany me to talk with the guy. He said he would be en route. Marcus was assigned to Coosa County for the second time in his career. He had started out here around 2008 and later transferred to Shelby County. He later returned to his home of Clay County but was assigned to Coosa. As of this writing, we have hired a new CEO for Coosa County and Marcus has now been reassigned to Clay County. If I don't miss my guess, he will finish out his career there.

Marcus soon arrived and we headed up WMA road 155 in separate trucks. We had gone about a mile and I was beginning to think this guy had moved on when I spotted his truck. I quickly realized there might be something wrong with the guy when I realized he was tending a small fire. While it wasn't necessarily unusual for someone to have a campfire, when the air temperature was close to ninety and the heat index was much more it wasn't the most common thing to see!

His truck was parked in the road and appeared to have quite a bit of equipment packed in it. I exited my truck and introduced myself and asked what the fellow was up to. He answered he was just cleaning up his camp. I asked if he knew he was on the WMA and he stated he did. I asked if he knew that having a fire on the WMA was illegal. His answer was an interesting one. He replied, "Is it get-a-ticket illegal or go-to-jail illegal?" I don't think I have ever had anyone answer a question just like that in the past!

I replied, it might not be either one. I asked if he had any firearms and he stated he had a rifle in his truck. I informed him that was illegal as well. I asked for his driver's license and he advised he did not have it with him but he knew his number. He recited the number and I told Marcus to keep an eye on him and I went to my truck and contacted the Coosa County Sheriff's Office (SO) dispatcher requesting a license and warrant check. The dispatcher ran the number and informed me that while the driver's license was valid, the man had a felony warrant for his arrest. I thanked them and exited my truck. I asked the fellow where his rifle was and he replied it was in a case on the back seat of his truck. The back seat was filled with garbage bags full of I didn't know what. However, I spotted the end of the gun case and removed the rifle. It was a .22-caliber rifle and it was loaded with a round in the chamber. I unloaded it and returned it to its case. I told the man that possessing the gun and having it loaded in the vehicle were also violations of WMA regulations. I asked where he was from and he replied he was sort of just living all over. He went on to say he had had a good job as a caregiver for an elderly man. He said was making good money but the man had gotten worse and then had died. I was surprised when he said it was probably his fault that the man had died since he was high all the time and didn't really take good care of the fellow. He said the man's wife was old and didn't know he was high all the time.

Unlike many of the folks we encountered on a regular basis this guy sure seemed to be an open book. I asked how he had ended up on the WMA and he said he was just looking for some place where he could get his head straight. He said he had been in the campground but had met some people there that he knew would take him down the wrong road again. He said he had found the Lord and was just looking for a place where he could read his Bible. He told me he had been talking with a preacher but he realized the preacher wanted him to see it his way and nobody else's. I told him preachers were often good guides but if they get away from what the Bible says you need to get away from them. I told him it was a wise move to recognize the wrong folks and not to reengage with them. However, unfortunately the WMA was not a place where he could get away from it all if the getting away included camping overnight.

During this whole time, I was deciding how to handle this situation. There were several things to consider. Obviously, he was going to have to be arrested on the felony warrant. That was not a problem but it would mean a lot of paperwork and headache. Next, he was in violation of at least three WMA regulations and probably more which needed to be addressed. Furthermore, he had a truck that evidently contained most of what he owned and I couldn't leave it in the middle of nowhere on the WMA and I hated to have it towed due to the cost involved. I decided to see if there was a deputy out that might could assist with the situation.

I returned to my truck and again contacted the SO dispatcher and asked if there was a deputy on duty that could assist me. They responded D205 was working. D205 was my longtime friend and coworker, Corporal Mike Rudd. Mike and I went way back. At one time we were both Little League umpires, which was probably a good training ground for a law enforcement officer! Mike had worked at a few different departments but had been with the Coosa SO for several years. He was a good friend and someone I knew I could count on whenever he was needed. I called Mike on the radio and asked if he could be en route to the double bridges boat launch. I explained we were in the WMA but would work our way down to him with an individual who had a felony warrant. He replied he would be en route.

I exited my truck and again approached our suspect. I told him we needed to make sure his fire was out and then we would work our way out of the area. His response was, "Did they not tell you I had a warrant or anything?" I wished he had not asked that. It was always a difficult time when someone asked a question like that because you never knew what their reaction was going to be. Even folks who knew very well they had a warrant would normally not act up until they knew you knew they had a warrant. I had to make a quick decision. I felt I had built a decent rapport with this guy up to this point and I knew if I lied to him now that rapport would be lost. Therefore, I told him yes, they did say he had a warrant and braced for his response. "Okay," was all he said. I told him we were going to move down to the paved road and we would discuss things down there. He again replied, "Okay," as if there was nothing to it. My first thought was to remove the rifle from his truck; however, I knew it was buried deep enough in the back seat he would not be able to access it while driving. Although it probably was not how it should have been handled, I decided not to mention it. I told him Marcus would lead the way and he could follow him and I would follow him. We each got in our trucks and headed out of the area.

It probably took about ten minutes to reach the old boat launch. When we arrived, I kept a close eye on the man as he exited his truck. There were no problems. I advised the man a deputy was en route to pick him up on a felony warrant. While that did not surprise him, he did immediately ask me which county the warrant was in. I advised it was in Autauga County. His immediate response was, "Okay, good, that's a lot better than Elmore County!" I replied, "Is that right?" and he responded, "Oh yeah, that Elmore County jail is rough." He said he was glad to have gotten out of there and he hoped he wouldn't have to go back when he got sentenced. It was at that point I realized there was possibly another charge here concerning a convicted felon being in possession of a firearm. However, not all felony convictions restricted gun rights and there were normally very few prosecutions for folks possessing rifles.

I explained the deputy would soon arrive and take him into custody and we needed to decide about his truck. He commented he had had his vehicle towed before and there wasn't much left in it when he got it back. I added to that the longer they keep it the more it costs and with him going to jail he couldn't know how long it would be there. I asked if he had anyone who could come to our location and get the truck. He replied his mom might come and get it. I asked if she had anyone she could bring that could drive it back. He said he thought so. I suggested we call her and get her en route if possible. He made the call and luckily she was there and said she would be on the way. I asked where she lived and he replied in Elmore County and added it would probably take her thirty minutes to get here. I thought to myself an hour would probably be more like it.

He took some money out of his pocket and left it on the front seat saying it was almost out of gas. He added, "The light has been on for a while." I asked what his warrant in Autauga County was for and he replied he was certain it was for drugs.

I told the man while he was in violation of several WMA regulations, I was going to write him warnings for possession of a firearm in the WMA and having a loaded firearm in a vehicle in the WMA. I explained that would conclude our business since the warnings did not require any follow-up on his part. Soon Corporal Rudd showed up and took the man into custody. I told the man I would wait until his mom arrived and turn the truck over to her.

As Marcus and I critiqued the incident and what we could have done differently or better the fellow's mom arrived to get the truck. We advised her the county had picked him up and was transporting him to Autauga County. She said that was better than Elmore County. She went on to say he had been beaten up in the Elmore County jail. Like her son, she was pretty talkative. She said she didn't know why he came up here. She said there was plenty of area around her home where he could camp out. I advised her the truck was on empty but he had left some money on the seat. I told her the nearest gas station was in Rockford and gave her directions and advised I would be coming behind her and would pick them up if they were to run out of gas.

She thanked us for staying with the truck and they were on their way. I gave the tickets to Marcus to turn in and we left as well. I couldn't help but think it was somewhat ironic that someone would go to the middle of nowhere and end up in more trouble there. However, as I thought it through I realized we didn't start his trouble, we just ended up in the middle of it. We also didn't add any of the charges we could have added to his problems. He had enough to worry with.

A couple of other things kept coming to mind as well. One was he had found the Lord. I could not help but think how his life would have been different if he had found the Lord years earlier. Chances are he would not be facing all he is now. In addition, I could not get past what he said about the preacher he had been talking to. I think if we would admit it, we probably all feel we are normally right about most things. I have to believe that if I didn't believe I was right about something, I would not continue in it. I know we can become very good at convincing ourselves we are correct and justifying what we do. I feel we have to guard against this self-justification. The man told me the preacher just wanted him to come to his church and not to listen to anyone else. I knew that sounded a little off but wasn't sure what he might be referring to. He went on to say he had told the preacher he had been talking with a couple of Jehovah's Witnesses and the preacher had told him he did not need to talk with them. While I agreed with the preacher, I wasn't sure how to proceed. However, I told him a preacher's job is to proclaim the true gospel and in order for him to know whether or not the preacher or anyone else was doing that, he needed to know the gospel. I told him if he would diligently study his Bible he would find it had all the answers.

I believe today we have many people who want nothing to do with any type of authority. Since Jesus is the ultimate authority, they want nothing to do with him. You have others who want to be religious but without it being authoritative or demanding anything from them. There are plenty of "preachers" out there who I feel cater to this type of person. One of the most egregious examples I ever heard of this was when I saw an "evangelist" on television and he said they had removed the cross from their sanctuary and from their teaching because the cross was negative to people. I can see that much of what the cross represents could be considered negative. Death, violence, hate, accusation, brokenness, and sin are all negative. However, the cross also represents life, peace, purity, wholeness, and forgiveness, which are all overwhelmingly positive. Furthermore, the cross represents finality. We all understand this life is finite. Unless Jesus decides to return in our lifetime we will all pass away. And here on earth that will be final. However, the cross demonstrates to us there is an eternity. We will all live on in eternity. Where we spend that eternity is up to us. Jesus willingly died on a cruel cross so we can spend eternity with him in heaven and avoid the devil's hell. He offers forgiveness and salvation. It's free for the asking. Therefore, I think the cross is worth including in my church. If anyone tells you the cross isn't a necessary part of the church, you better find another church!

I never saw this fellow again. I pray he kept reading his Bible and found the answers he needed. I was encouraged by his realization that the folks he hung around with definitely had an effect on him. Unfortunately, several folks don't realize that until it is eternally too late. We all must remember, we are responsible for all we do. Although today's culture tries to make us believe that isn't true, it is and always will be. The wages of sin is death but the gift of God is eternal life. Choose wisely, choose Jesus!

Now He Knows

I HAVE PROVIDED MANY ACCOUNTS of incidences of people lying to me. This is likely because it has happened so often I have come to believe some folks would rather climb a tree and tell a lie than to stand on the ground and tell the truth. It doesn't seem to matter whether you are working checking hunters, fishermen, or drivers, or umpiring a Little League ball game. Some of those folks are just prone to lie to you.

I have trained many law enforcement officers and I always try to impress on them the vital need to be able to read people. There are many nonverbal cues people will exhibit that will tell you a lot if you are paying attention. When speaking with officers and others I try to help them understand that everyone reads people every day.

Recently I observed a fellow fishing from the creek bank. He was feverishly casting and reeling in his line. I wasn't sure what he was trying to catch but by the way he was operating his equipment, I knew whatever he might catch would have to be able to move pretty dang fast to catch his lure. I walked up to within a few feet of the man. I knew he had seen me pull up in my truck and he had seen me exit the truck and walk toward him. However, he had not turned toward me nor did he slow down on his casting and retrieving. This is the type of body language I'm talking about. In my experience, this lack of acknowledgment of my presence is often indicative of someone who is in violation in some way. I've never really figured out what exactly they think is going to happen. Do they think if they don't acknowledge my being there, maybe I will just turn and walk away? This fisherman and I were the only two people present so I do not think he was waiting on me to move on to someone else. I'm not sure what he was thinking would happen.

I decided a comment would be appropriate so I said, "By the way you are casting, I don't think you have caught your limit yet." As he made another cast he told me he had not caught anything and asked, "What do people catch fish on around here?" I told him I had seen folks have decent luck with a white rooster tail. He reeled his line in and grabbed hold of the bait and turned and showed it to me. It was a gold rooster tail. I told him I didn't see why that wouldn't work. He said he had tried it here and across the road and had not caught anything. I felt, with his line reeled in, it was a good time to ask if I could see his fishing license. I felt certain this was the question he had been trying to avoid by not acknowledging my being there. He looked at me with a straight face and said, "I didn't know I needed one." I asked how old he was and he replied that he was thirty-six years old. I told him any Alabama resident between the ages of sixteen and sixty-five who was fishing in the public waters of the state was required to have a fishing license. He repeated he did not know that. I have always tried to teach young officers that our job is very much one of education. This day was no different and due to the efforts of myself and our district judge, this guy can now consider himself educated.

Knight's First Big Night

I DON'T KNOW ABOUT EVERYONE, but I have never forgotten the first case I ever made nor my first night hunting case. When I entered this profession as a wildlife biologist with law enforcement authority, my contact with law enforcement was receiving a speeding ticket on the way to college one morning, getting stopped by a game warden for spotlighting back when spotlighting was legal, and riding on a patrol with a game warden one night while in graduate school. The first time I ever appeared in court was as an arresting officer. I assure you it has been a long wild ride since then! A ride I have survived only by the grace of a loving God!

I had been working for three days when I made my first arrest. It was carrying a loaded firearm in a vehicle in Coosa Wildlife Management Area. I remember the subject's name and where the stop took place. I also remember the gravity of the situation. I quickly realized the authority to take someone's freedom from them was an awesome responsibility.

Today, more than thirty-seven years since it occurred, I can still vividly recall my first night hunting arrests. It was a little scary and a lot exhilarating. I've never forgotten and hope I never will. You need to understand this was when night hunting was rampant in rural Coosa County. I guess you could say this was during my on-the-job training. At that time our department did not have a formal field training program. I was very fortunate the two officers in the county were willing to show me the ropes so to speak. During this time, the wildlife section, which I was a part of, and the law enforcement section, which the officers were a part of, did not get along. It was for the most part a contentious relationship. Again, it was my great fortune that the officers would help me and help me they did and I continue to be grateful.

My first pair of night hunters shot the pitiful little decoy with a 16-gauge shotgun loaded with six shot. We had a short pursuit in which they ended up in the ditch. The next guy blasted the Styrofoam wonder with three rounds from a 30-30 rifle. It was a great night and I was hooked!

Months later I attended the police academy. One of my instructors asked who I worked for and when I replied Game and Fish, he replied, "You're just asking to get killed." I would learn what he was talking about. I totally embraced the law enforcement aspect of the job and thoroughly enjoyed it. I like to feel I was good at it. I know I was good enough that it earned me the ire of "fellow" officers. When I was working enforcement in addition to all of my wildlife biologist duties and was outperforming the full-time officers, neither they nor their supervisors were happy about it. I remember the day in the Hollins WMA when an officer came in and said he had made some hunting-without-a-permit cases that morning. I said that's great. He went on to say the arrests that morning had brought him up to his yearly average of cases. My counterpart, Gene Carver, asked him how many that was and he happily replied fourteen. I know my mouth fell open. Gene looked at me and asked how many cases I had and I replied I wasn't going to say. The officer looked at me and asked if I had more than that and I answered that I did. He asked how many I had and I reluctantly told him I had fifty. He just shrugged his shoulders. That didn't win you many friends. I was not in a competition, I was just doing the best job I could. I was in a target-rich environment. As I said by the grace of God I've survived over four thousand arrests and many harrowing experiences. Vehicle chases at 137 miles per hour and the realization of hunters looking at me through the scope on their rifle. It's been wild.

Now in my thirty-seventh year, I am once again training a new officer. I retired after thirty years and came back six months later as a member of the law enforcement section Special Task Force. It has been fun. I very much enjoy training new officers. I feel like I have a lot to teach them. I know they feel like I have a lot of crazy stories! I hope they will glean through the stories and come up with the nuggets that are lying in there!

As I was about to start my thirty-seventh year, a new officer was hired for Coosa County. Like most of the ones I had seen for the past several years, he looked like he was about twelve years old. I know he thought I looked like I was eighty! I was thankful to have him there. We had some things in common in that he had received a wildlife degree. He got it at Auburn but I didn't hold that against him. Hey, not everyone can go to Mississippi State! I digress.

Conservation Officer Trainee Justin Knight graduated from the police academy on December 1 and hit the ground running. Well, as much so as someone who is finishing up a field officer training program.

One of the last requirements of the training program was that the new officer would work with the captain for about a week. This would allow the supervisor to let the new officer know what they expected and how they wanted things done and allowed them to share insights on the job. On one of the days spent with the captain, they had received a tip from someone they did not know at a local restaurant about a place where there might be some night hunting taking place. Not having anything any better, they decided to try it. They went to the area and located a greenfield that looked like it might be alluring to some lowdown scoundrel bent on breaking the law. They returned that night and sure enough heard a shot off in the distance. While that was exciting, most of the time there isn't much you can do with a shot in the distance.

The next week, CEO Knight was released for solo duty. He hit the ground running. He had told me about hearing the nighttime shot and told me a lot of the area had been clear-cut. I took a ride down and looked at the area. I had worked the area several times in the past with some success. We called the area Wayside since the only prominent feature was the Wayside Baptist Church. There had been a lot of timber harvesting taking place and I even saw a decent buck in one of the clear-cuts while I was down there. I checked an area where I had parked in the past working night hunting and decided it would once again be a decent vantage point. I called Knight and told him we would work it that weekend.

We met in the area the next Friday night. There was enough room for both trucks in the hiding spot so we parked side by side. We had not been there very long when off to the southeast we heard a shot that wasn't that far off. I immediately began going through the map in my mind trying to decipher where it likely originated from. I told Justin a good rule of thumb was if you were consistently hearing shots in an area, eventually they would likely migrate to your location. At least it's a lot better spot than where you haven't been hearing anything!

The next Saturday night found us once again in the same location. We decided to take both of our vehicles so we could cover more area. Although he had been released to patrol on his own, it was still a good idea to have him close to another officer.

212

We had decided to set up on County Roads 36 and 45 in the Wayside community in south Coosa County right on the Elmore County line. We were approximately a mile apart with Justin monitoring the large greenfield he and the captain had worked and myself watching a segment of the area that had been clear-cut. We both settled in and made sure our radios would work on car-to-car, which meant our transmissions did not go through the repeater and could only be heard a short distance. Things were working well and we settled in to begin our vigil.

We had been in place maybe fifteen minutes when I observed a white Chevrolet pickup with a light bar in the grill and pulling a small trailer as it passed my location going northbound on the county road. Within approximately ten seconds I heard a shot. I called CEO Knight and told him to come on. I pursued the truck and quickly caught up with it. I did not immediately stop the vehicle as I was hoping for CEO Knight to catch up and see how things worked. Soon I could see his headlights quickly approaching. I activated my blue lights and the vehicle pulled to the right side of the road. I radioed the Coosa County Sheriff's Office (CCSO) dispatcher that I was stopping a white Chevrolet pickup but the tag was obstructed by a trailer. I exited my vehicle and told the driver, the sole occupant of the truck, to place his hands out the window. I moved far enough to the side that I could get the tag number and called it in to the dispatch. I heard CCSO Sgt. Mike Rudd advise that he was en route to my location. I always appreciated a backup unit, although it was a rarity in our rural county.

CEO Knight had exited his truck and had taken up a support position on the passenger side of the truck. I asked the driver, Barry Snowden, if he possessed a weapon and he stated there was a shotgun in the back floorboard. I had Mr. Snowden exit the vehicle and place his hands on the side of the truck. When he opened the driver's door, I immediately spotted what appeared to be a spent shotgun shell in the driver's side floorboard. I asked CEO Knight to pat him down for weapons. While he did that, I removed the 12-gauge shotgun from the truck and took it to my vehicle where I unloaded two buckshot shells from it. I returned to the truck and asked Mr. Snowden if there were any more weapons in the truck. He quickly replied it was not his truck and he was not sure. A cursory look did not reveal any other weapons; however, there was a spotlight and two flashlights in plain view in the front passenger seat. I returned to Mr. Bowden and advised him of his rights by reading him the Miranda warning. He stated he understood.

At that point, he immediately stated he thought I was after the small silver Honda car that had blown past him at a high rate of speed. I quickly replied there were no other vehicles on the road. He again stated the silver Honda had come out from the church and had flown around him. I gave him "the look" and I told him I knew that didn't happen. I let that hang in the air for a few seconds and looking him directly in the eye I said, "I was at the church!" I hoped CEO Knight was listening intently because if he was he probably heard something go "pffft" and I think it came from Mr. Snowden's pants!

I sensed this was the time to strike while the iron was hot and I advised Mr. Snowden of the elements of a night hunting violation and told him he fulfilled all of them. He stated he wasn't night hunting. I told him that was why we had court but I had been doing this for a long time and I felt certain he would be convicted. He pondered that for a few seconds and then stated, "I did it. I shot at a deer." Mr. Snowden gave me the details and I wrote out his statement and he signed it. I asked if he had a permit to hunt any property in the area and he stated he did not. He was arrested for hunting at night, hunting from a public road, and hunting by aid of a vehicle.

Deputies Rudd and Payton arrived on the scene to assist. A review of his driver's license revealed it was revoked. I advised him he would not be allowed to leave there driving. I told him since he had been cooperative, if he had a licensed driver who could come and get him and the truck, we would not have it towed. Deputy Rudd commented that he had recently had a truck with a trailer towed and it had cost $800! Mr. Snowden said he could definitely have someone come and get him. He got on the phone and started lining things up.

While he was making his call, I called Captain Grady Myers who, while he was the captain in another district, lived just a few miles from our current location. Knowing he had made the acquaintance of many members of the Snowden family, I wanted to see if he was familiar with Barry. I reached him and told him I had Barry Snowden stopped in Coosa County and was wondering if he was familiar with him. His response was classic. He said he had caught so many members of that family, he could no longer tell them apart. He then added, "But if you think he did something, I assure you he did!" I told him we had hooked him up for night hunting just above the county line and he replied, "Good deal."

Mr. Snowden was allowed to sign his own bond. I advised him he was not being charged with driving while revoked, hunting without a permit, hunting without a license, or hunting without a harvest record but that all of those charges could be brought within the next year. He stated he understood.

Soon thereafter the designated driver arrived. I found it pretty funny when the man got out of his vehicle and the first thing he said to Mr. Snowden was, "Man, I told you you would get caught if you tried this mess up here!"

As the two men drove away, I turned to CEO Knight and told him now was the time for high fives! To say he was excited was an understatement. Of course, I was somewhat elated myself. We thanked the deputies for their assistance and headed for home.

Prior to the court date, I wrote out a court preparation outline for CEO Knight. It included questions such as what gives the Commissioner of Conservation the authority to promulgate regulations and what gives us the authority to enforce them. I also told him to write a detailed narrative concerning the arrests and to develop a succinct testimony. He did a good job on all of it.

The court date finally arrived. I had told CEO Knight I figured Mr. Snowden would be appointed an attorney and their first order of business would be to ask that the cases be continued until the next month. I advised him I had all of our evidence ready for them so there was no more "discovery" for them to have to wait on.

Mr. Snowden's name was called and we all approached the judge's bench. The judge asked if he wanted an attorney and he advised he did. The judge gave him the paperwork to fill out to see if he met the hardship criteria so he could be appointed an attorney. He completed the paperwork and returned it to the judge. The judge reviewed it and told him he would appoint someone. There were several attorneys in the courtroom who would take appointments. I had told CEO Knight who I hoped he would appoint. The primary reason I hoped he would appoint this particular attorney was because she wasn't a jerk. I couldn't say that for several others that were eligible! Of course, it didn't hurt that I had known this girl since she was a small child. Lo and behold she was appointed. However, she quickly handed it off to her subordinate who immediately came to me and said she would need a continuance so they could acquire discovery. I reached in my folder and handed her the packet and told her that was all of it. She had a blank look on her face and turned and walked away. I might mention I've known her since she was born as well. I understand they have a job to do, but I can't help but think things could move faster. She returned and advised they still were going to need a continuance so she could review the laws and regulations and I told her I understood.

The next month we were once again back in the court room. Seeing how the defendant had been assigned an attorney, this in effect moved him to the end of the court docket. This meant we would be there most of the morning. There was also another wrinkle thrown in. I was stopped by court room security when I entered the court room and advised there was a need for additional alertness today in that there would be a witness in the court room who was expected to testify in a preliminary hearing for a murder trial. The court had received word that the family of the murder suspect had vowed to kill the witness. Therefore, all of the officers in the court room needed to be on high alert. It just kept getting better!

After working through the docket, the judge announced the court would take a short recess in order for lawyers to meet with clients and the district attorney (DA) and hopefully settle some cases. During this time the assistant district attorney approached me and wanted to know if we were okay with dropping one of the charges against Mr. Snowden and I told him we were willing to drop the hunting by the aid of a vehicle charge. He said he would get it set up.

Court was placed back in session and the judge began hearing settlements. At this point, the attorney for Mr. Snowden approached us and asked if there was any way we could reduce the amount of the fines in the case. She advised due to his financial situation they were not going to be charging any attorney's fees and the DA had said he would drop the court costs. I consulted with CEO Knight and asked what he thought about us getting a guilty plea in every case but dropping the fine in the hunting from the road case. This would decrease the amount by $1,350. He agreed and I informed the attorneys. They were very appreciative and I told them we only did it because they were our favorites!

I explained to CEO Knight that court was often a give-and-take situation and sometimes you were giving and sometimes someone else was. I told him if an attorney was willing to work with me I was willing to work with them. However, I also reminded him the best way to be in a strong negotiating position was to have an airtight case and you only did that by dotting your i's and crossing your t's. I also reminded him even the very best prepared case could be lost, but it wouldn't happen very often.

This case occurred just over thirty-six years after my first big night. It has been my good fortune to be involved in over 230 night hunting cases since then. Each one has been exciting. I seriously doubt CEO Knight will ever see that many night hunting cases since it just does not occur as much as it used to. However, I know he is actively looking for his next one and that's what it takes to find one. CEO Knight might possibly forget this case, but I don't think I will! I'm not sure if the thrill was as great on this one as the first one, but it was pretty dang good! Good luck CEO Knight, now you know how it's done. Go get 'em!

A Well-Fed Dog!

MANY TIMES, I HAVE WRITTEN that one of my favorite parts of my job was not knowing what would happen next. It was not unusual to leave home with the intent to work in the northwest part of the county and end up answering a call in the county to the south. Many times, your planned day or night would end up not resembling anything you had planned. However, there were some things that pretty much happened on schedule. One of those was that night hunting of deer would start before the legal deer season started.

While I'm sure we had folks who hunted at night year-round, things seemed to pick up a good bit in October and early November. I reasoned that once the bow season began and people could legally possess a deer, they ramped up their illegal activity which in turn began to generate complaints.

While many night hunting complaints were little more than someone had heard a shot somewhere, every once in a while, you would get some helpful details. I received an email from our district office stating someone, who wanted to remain anonymous, had reported someone night hunting on County Road 157 in the Richville community. The caller had given some pretty specific details. They stated someone was spotlighting between 3:00 a.m. and 5:00 p.m. They said the culprit was driving a white pickup truck. They went on to say we should not tell anyone about it because if we did we would likely be talking to the one who was doing it. That was some interesting info.

I have written several times about early morning night hunting complaints. I did not mind working until two in the morning. I had no problem coming out at four in the morning and working the rest of the day. However, for some reason working from two to four in the morning was difficult for me. I've done it, but I didn't like it. Well, obviously this complaint was right in the middle of that!

The warning that if we told someone we would likely be talking to the offender was interesting and aggravating. While I can understand a complainant not wanting to reveal their identity, when they won't tell you who the violator is it makes catching them a lot more difficult. Fortunately, I was 90 percent sure I knew who the complainant was and I knew who he was talking about. Unfortunately, I knew the fellow he was referring to would not be spotlighting or hunting by the complainant's house. Now I will assure you there are very few people who I believe would not break the law. I don't put much past a lot of folks, however, I felt 99 percent certain the person they were pointing the finger at was not the one doing it. Years earlier, he would be the prime suspect; however, the Lord had made a genuine change in his life. I knew him well and I ruled him out. Don't think that isn't a monumental statement because experience had taught me not to put anything past folks.

I contacted my partner, Marcus Rowell, and informed him of the complaint and asked if he wanted to work it with me. He said he did and I told him I thought we ought to try it on Saturday morning. He said he would be there.

I set my clock for 2:00 a.m. It was hard to do that. As often happens, I was awake and watching the clock. I turned off the alarm so it would not wake my wife and I got ready and headed for the reported area. I knew the area well and had a pretty good idea of a good place to work.

A friend of mine owned some property that bordered the road. There was an old house on the north side of the road and about a two-acre field alongside the road. On the south side was also a field and another old house with a barn behind it. No one had lived in either house for a very long time. My plan was to pull up beside the barn and from there I should be able to monitor both fields without being seen.

I arrived at the barn at about 2:45. I backed up beside the barn and looked things over. Things always look different in the dark. I talked Marcus into another hiding spot about a half mile east of my location. I got out and covered my windshield with my black blanket. While doing so I heard a slight noise behind me and was a little surprised when a dog came into view. While the dog did not appear to be aggressive, it did seem to be a little curious about who was invading its space. I was also a little curious about what the dog was doing out here a mile from the nearest house. I got in my truck and began my surveillance.

At 3:30 a.m. I heard what I thought was a vehicle coming my way from the east. Soon I could see headlights moving slowly along the road. I thought this might be some good information after all. I watched as the vehicle slowly drove past the two fields. When it got directly in front of me I saw the brake lights come on. The vehicle slowed to a stop in front of the old house and barn. It sat there for about a minute and then turned around and drove back the way it had come. No spotlighting, no nothing. We stayed until about 5:30 and did not have another vehicle. We headed for home.

Three nights later I decided to give the area another try. Once again, I was set up and monitoring the area before 3:00 a.m. Once again, the dog came and greeted me when I arrived. At precisely

3:30 a small pickup truck came down the road in front of me. The driver pulled to the exact same spot as before and stopped. The vehicle sat still for about a minute and then turned around and left just like before.

I sat there scratching my head trying to figure out just what this guy was up to. He wasn't shining a spotlight as reported, but he was definitely up to something. I stayed until about five and headed for home.

I was now becoming obsessed with this situation. Three nights later I again headed to the area. I pulled into my hiding spot and began putting my blanket over my windshield so the moon wouldn't be reflecting off of it. The dog came over to check me out and I remembered I had some dog treats in the door of my truck so I retrieved one and gave to the dog. I had come to understand the dog evidently lived at the barn. She was friendly and was not wild in the least.

I began my visual and things began to play out in the same way once again. However, there were a couple of differences. The truck was actually early, arriving at 3:25. The truck slowly rolled past my location and stopped in the exact same spot as the previous two nights. However, instead of turning around, in about a minute the truck drove off in the same direction it had been going. I had been surprised that the truck had not been continuing down the road on the previous nights. Like most of our county, this road was scarcely populated with two residences at the east end of the road and no more for the next four miles. It was an ideal place to night hunt. I stayed until about 5:00 a.m. and once again headed for home, scratching my head.

Many ideas had gone through my mind. I thought the driver might be using night vision to look in the fields. However, he had not stopped by the fields. Where he had stopped was fairly close to a security light which I thought would probably not be ideal for trying to see through a night scope. Since the first night I had considered that the driver might be using their headlights to shine alongside the road when they were turning around. I thought of several things but none of them seemed right.

A few nights later I was once again in position and just like clockwork at 3:30 the truck came down the road. The driver passed my location and came to a stop. He sat there for about a minute, turned around and went back the way he had come. I decided this had gone on too long. I felt the turning around and shining the headlights off the side of the road was enough probable cause to stop the truck.

I pulled out behind the truck and was quickly upon it. I ran the tag through the Coosa SO dispatch. They gave me the name of the registered owner. I advised dispatch of my location and told them I would be stopping the vehicle. Although I had done this hundreds of times before, it still went through my mind that I was literally in the middle of nowhere, I was likely the only law enforcement officer working in the whole county and in all likelihood this fellow had a firearm.   I activated my blue lights and the vehicle immediately pulled to the side of the road. I exited my truck and approached. I told the driver to raise his hands and he complied. I eased on up toward the window and looked in the truck with my flashlight. I noticed there was a small dog in the passenger seat. I asked the driver to place his hands on the steering wheel and he complied. I asked if he had any weapons and he replied he had a pistol on his side. I advised him not to touch it.

I informed the driver the reason I was stopping him was I had seen him turning around back up the road. I asked, "What were you doing back there?"

He did not hesitate when he said, "I'm feeding a dog that lives back there." I must admit, I didn't see that coming!

I replied, "Feeding a dog?" and he said, "Yes, it lives back there at that barn." I asked the man where he lived and he replied County Road 173. I quickly calculated in my mind that was about ten miles from our current location. I said, "Let me get this straight. You are driving ten miles one way to feed a dog that isn't yours?" He replied, "Yes sir and I've been doing it for about a year." Once again, I was taken back by this information.

While I was baffled by this situation I decided to try and solicit some more information. I asked for his driver's license and he produced it. I asked the fellow where he worked and he told me he was retired from REA. REA was how most everyone referred to the Rural Electric Cooperative, whose name has changed a few times. Today it is known as the Central Alabama Electric Coop. In much of our rural area, they are the power company. It just so happened one of my best friends was also an REA retiree. I told the man I appreciated his cooperation and he was free to go. I returned to my truck, still scratching my head.

The next morning, I contacted my friend and inquired about the fellow. He immediately told me the fellow was a good man and asked where I had run into him. I told him I had talked with him at about 3:30 in the morning on County Road 157. He asked what he was doing and I replied he said he was down there feeding a dog! My friend did not hesitate and said, "Oh yeah, he's all about dogs." He said he had known of him finding a dog on the side of the road and taking it to the vet, getting its shot, and so forth. He said the fellow did not spare any expense when it came to helping a dog. I told him I appreciated the information. I therefore concluded the man's story was legitimate.

As I thought about this situation, I put a pencil to it. This guy was driving approximately twenty miles a day to feed a dog that did not belong to him. Not to mention the cost of the food, the gas alone is more than $1,000 a year!

By the way, the dog in this story belongs to another friend of mine who maintains food and water for the dog. I guess you could say I was the loser in this story in that I spent several hours from two to five in the morning staking out a property in order to apprehend a Good Samaritan dog lover who rose at three o'clock every morning to drive twenty miles to feed a dog that did not belong to him. Now that's a dog lover!

I phoned my friend back and asked if he would mind contacting his fellow retiree and give him my address and tell him there are a couple of dogs there that might need to be fed! As I have said on many occasions, and as this story once again proves, you can't make this stuff up!

Just Trying to See a Big Buck

COMPLAINTS ARE MOST DEFINITELY A MIXED BAG. Conservation enforcement officers (CEOs) receive complaints in many ways. It may be a phone call, a text, an email, a note left on your windshield, or it may come through the sheriff's office or police department. You may receive it in person at the gas station, at church, at the gym, at Little League, or maybe at Walmart. Suffice it to say it might come from anywhere.

Complaints may be cryptic, detailed, sketchy, true, false, accurate, or hard to comprehend. Some give you all you need and some don't give you enough to warrant looking into. As I said it's a mixed bag. One of the complaints we dislike the most is the untimely complaint. I always told folks if they witnessed something to call me right then even if it was two o'clock in the morning. Unfortunately, a lot of folks would not call until the next day or worse yet until after the season was over. There wasn't much we could do then.

I received a call from the Coosa County Sheriff's Office (CCSO) dispatcher who told me Angela Smith had called in a complaint stating someone was hunting on their property both late at night and early in the morning. Seeing how we were over halfway through the deer season, that was definitely something we were interested in. They gave me the phone number and I immediately called. I did not receive an answer so I identified myself as the game warden, left my number, and asked that she call me. In our current day, I'm sure you have received a call from an unknown number and you did not answer it. That was common. However, most of the time, when I left a message the folks would pick up before I hung up. If that didn't happen I would normally receive a call shortly thereafter. That did not happen in this instance. I did not receive a call back at all. The next day I called the dispatcher back and made sure I had recorded the number correctly. I had. He said he would call them back and give them my number as well. I asked if he had the address of the caller and he provided it to me. Still no call.

I looked the address up on the GIS map and found there was a large field adjacent to the county road. I decided I would go to the property and see what it looked like. Finding a hiding place from which you could observe an area where you had information that illegal hunting was taking place often wasn't as simple as you might think. A good observation point was often hard to come by.

I arrived at the area, which was a field probably twenty acres in size and directly adjacent to the paved county road. While that was good, there was a problem. Due to a railroad track that was maybe thirty-five yards on the other side of the road from the field, there was nowhere to sit and observe the field from that side of the road. Therefore, the only vantage point was in the field. As you can imagine, when you are trying to apprehend someone shooting into a field, it isn't always the best idea to sit in that field! Unfortunately, that is sometimes the only option and this was looking like one of those times.

There was a road, actually a driveway, that ran through the field. About 150 yards off the paved road and adjacent to the driveway was a thick stand of pine trees on one side of the road and a small shed on the other side. I looked it over and decided sitting between the two would provide a little cover but I still didn't really like it. Another major problem was it would be very difficult to come out on someone without them seeing us coming and getting a good jump on us if they decided to run. But as often was the case, it was the only game in town.

I contacted CEO Knight and advised him of the complaint and told him I thought we should give the area a try that weekend. He was ready and willing. I went by and picked him up and we went to the site. On the way I explained the problems with sitting on the same side of the road that you expected a violator to shoot on. I also discussed that we would just take one vehicle this time since there was only one place to sit but we might locate another spot down the road so we could spread out the next time.

We arrived at the spot and he immediately liked the place. He commented this looked more like where someone would hunt than where we had been working. I understood what he was talking about. I figure most people would think that someone looking to shoot a deer at night would ride around checking fields to see if there were any deer using them. While that is the way a lot of folks do it, that works fine when you have a county with a bunch of fields. That wasn't Coosa County. The last time I had looked at some statistics for our county we were 92 percent forested. Fields on the side of the road were rare. While we definitely had folks who shot deer in fields at night, what we normally encountered was what we had coined "ditch shooters." It seemed that most of the deer in our county enjoyed feeding in the ditch alongside the road. If you don't believe that you could contact our insurance agents and see how many deer were hit by vehicles in our county each year! Also, a deer in the ditch was normally an easy shot and could be scooped up and gone with in a hurry. Lastly, since deer might be in any ditch anywhere in the county, the chance of a game warden being nearby was slim to none. I must admit it was nice to have a field to watch, it just didn't happen very often.

We sat on the field until past midnight with very little traffic. As I have mentioned many times, night hunting work was extremely boring, until it wasn't. However, it did allow plenty of time for me to bore my rookie partner with stories from the past thirty-six years! Despite not having any luck, the rookie really liked the place and said we definitely needed to try it again.

The next weekend we decided to give the field another try. We pulled down the driveway and when I turned into the field to back into our hiding spot, my headlights lit up six deer standing in the field. Of course, they ran off, but it was still a good sign. We got backed in and rolled down the windows.

We had not been there for five minutes when we heard our first vehicle coming from our left. As soon as the car reached the field, I saw what looked like a light in the car window. While it was obviously a light, it was not shining in the field. As I said "What is that?" the beam of the light started sweeping across the field. My young partner nearly shouted, "He's shining!" I cranked the truck and started down the long driveway as quickly as possible with my headlights off. Departmental policy is we cannot get on the public road at night without our headlights on. Now I'm sure some of you are thinking, You have to have a policy to tell you that? I'm sure it will surprise you to know when I started work, it was very common to drive without headlights at night. Many night hunters were caught when they shot with the game warden sitting in the road behind them with no lights on. Sometimes after having followed them for miles! However, while it was effective, it was not a very safe thing to do and was eventually stopped.

When we reached the road, I turned my headlights on and started toward the vehicle, which had a pretty good jump on me. I could tell I was gaining on the vehicle; however, I knew we were nearing an intersection and I told my partner to watch for other vehicles if we hadn't caught him before we reached the crossroads. I decided I was close enough to activate my lights and did so in hopes he would stop prior to the crossroad.

The driver pulled to the side of the road at the intersection. I radioed the CCSO dispatcher and advised we were stopping a white Honda car and gave her the location. We exited the truck and gave the driver, the sole occupant of the vehicle, the loud verbal command to place his hands out the window. He immediately complied. I approached on the driver's side. I identified myself as the game warden and asked if he had any weapons in his vehicle. He advised he had a pistol but he had a permit for it. I asked where it was and he advised it was in the floorboard. I advised him to keep his hands up as I moved up and opened his door. I told him to keep his hands up, step out, and move to the trunk and place his hands on it. When he got to the trunk he looked at me and said, "Man, I was just trying to see a big buck, I wasn't night hunting." I told him we would talk in a minute.

I asked CEO Knight to pat him down for weapons and I returned to his vehicle and retrieved his handgun, which was in the driver's side floorboard. I also grabbed the spotlight he had laid in the rear seat. I carried the items back to my truck and removed the loaded magazine from the pistol and a round from the barrel.

I moved back to the suspect and asked if he had any identification and he handed me his driver's license and pistol permit. I advised him of his rights by reading him the Miranda warning. He stated he understood his rights. He again stated he was only trying to see a big buck that had been reported to be using the field. I asked where he was coming from and he replied he had been at a bonfire with family and friends and someone there had said they had seen a big buck hanging out in the field alongside the road. He said he decided he would shine the field and see if he could spot the big buck but he had no intention of shooting the deer. I told him he fulfilled the elements of a night hunting case by being in an area where deer were known to frequent at night, having a light source, possessing a weapon, and that combined with the overt act of shining the light in the field constituted a night hunting violation. He stated he understood. I asked if he realized it was illegal to shine the field with the spotlight and he said he did. I asked if he had a permit to hunt the property or a hunting license and he said he did not.

Although he was the first vehicle we had seen that evening, during the short time we had been out with him four vehicles stopped to ask him if everything was okay. This was somewhat unusual; however, I felt I understood it. Unfortunately, this was the day after the video of the beating death of a black motorist in Memphis had been released. In response to this, various groups had decided to call for "a night of rage" where law enforcement would be targeted. With this being true, the cars stopping at the scene were of extra concern. I advised CEO Knight to keep an eye on the traffic while I quickly took the man's information and statement and told him we would be back in touch with him. I returned his unloaded handgun and spotlight to him and allowed him to leave.

We returned to our hiding spot and I explained to my partner I felt it was the safest for all involved for us to conclude the stop and handle the paperwork later. He asked if we could legally do that and I explained we actually had a year from the date of the offense to bring the charges. I told him it would have been much easier and simpler to have written the tickets right then but I felt it was prudent to handle it as we did. He agreed the number of people coming by and stopping was a little unnerving.

The following Monday we went to the clerk's office to obtain warrants for the charges of hunting at night, hunting from the road, and hunting by the aid of a vehicle. We were about to find it would have been much easier to have written the tickets on-scene. We learned our clerk's office had recently changed to a new warrant system called e-warrant. They explained using e-warrant we would not be able to use our normal procedure of allowing the arrestee to sign their own bond but we would have to place the defendant in jail. This was a headache we would prefer to avoid. They said there was an alternative in that we could take out a summons which could be served on the subject without taking him to jail. We opted for that option. They prepared the summons and we left the courthouse.

The next morning, I was contacted by the clerk who told me we needed to return the summons and get warrants. I called CEO Knight and advised him he needed to go back to the courthouse and switch the summons for warrants. Later that day he contacted me saying he had gone to the courthouse and turned in the summons. They had issued warrants and then before he left they had decided to go back with the summons. Hey, it was new to all of us and he were just trying to get it right!

That evening I received an interesting call from CEO Knight. He explained he had received a call from the defendant who said he had been contacted and told there were warrants out for his arrest. This quickly got our attention. Knight had asked where he had heard that and he said a police officer had contacted him and told him. Obviously, if true, this was a total breach of ethics not to mention how incredibly dangerous it had the potential to be. I did not feel this would have resulted in a terribly dangerous situation since the defendant knew we were obtaining the warrants and would be arresting him. However, this was a very troubling development.

We set up a meeting with the suspect for the next morning. He arrived shortly after the arranged time and we took care of the paperwork. We then asked a few questions about the officer contacting him. He said the officer had called him and asked what he had done. He said he asked what he was talking about and he told him there were warrants out for his arrest. The suspect said the officer told him it was something that had happened on County Road 81 and he said he then understood he was talking about the hunting offenses. I asked why he thought the officer had called him and he said he had called him in the past when he had child support warrant for him. We made sure he knew when the court date was and told him we would see him there.

The next month we were in court and our defendant was seated on the front row. The judge worked through the docket and finally reached the man's name. The man approached the bench and CEO Knight and I met him there. The district judge advised the man of his charges and asked how he pled. The man replied, "Not guilty." The judge asked the man if he would like to be represented by an attorney and he replied, "No, I just want to get it over with." The judge had him sign a waiver of counsel. He then had each of us raise our hand and be sworn. He looked at CEO Knight and said, "Since you are listed as the arresting officer, tell me what happened." This would be the first time that CEO Knight actually had to give a testimony in court. Although his voice sounded a little shaky, he did a good job of telling what had occurred. The judge asked the defendant if he had any questions for the officer and he said he did not. He asked if he had anything he wanted to say and the man told him he realized he was in violation but it was not his intent to shoot a deer, he was just trying to see one. The judge commented a pistol would kill a deer like any other gun and found the man guilty and ordered the minimum fine and court costs in each case and revoked his hunting privileges for three years. It was a hefty price tag and the judge told him he would allow him some time to pay it. The man said he could pay $100 each month. The judge advised him it would be $100 every month and the first month he failed to pay he could start serving his ninety days in jail! The man stated he understood and left the courtroom.

I must admit I hated to see this man get hit so hard. Our plan had been to work out an agreement with his attorney, which would have saved him some money. However, when he waived his right to counsel, it took that option off the table. I feel certain we don't have to worry about him shining a field again even if someone tells him there's a moose standing in it!

A Dang Good Un

As the handcuffed man stood at the front of his truck he uttered a familiar statement: "I've never done anything like this before." For some reason, maybe thirty-seven years of doing this, I had some suspicion that statement might not be the truth!

Lt. Jerry Fincher contacted me and said he wanted to try a road hunting detail. I had an inkling where it might be. For some reason, we game wardens tend to work in areas where we have repeatedly caught violators. Most folks have a favorite spot and one of Jerry's favorites was ironically called Glover's Ferry.

I have no idea how many folks he apprehended hunting there both day and night but I do know it was a lot. When he said he wanted to try it with our two brand-new game wardens in tow, I hoped it would turn out well once again. I was not disappointed.

While setting up a road hunting detail is pretty straight-forward, there are several moving parts to it. You hope to have a site without any side roads that might allow a violator to escape. Glover's Ferry fit the bill in that it was a straight stretch of road that could effectively be blocked on each end with no way out. Another great attribute was there was usually no shortage of deer standing in the fields along the road. It was a good place.

Lt. Fincher, Sgt. Bassett, CEOs Nixon, Knight, Davis, and myself all assembled at our staging point and Jerry laid out the detail. He and Knight would be on the ground with the deer decoy. I would be set up on the south end of the road and the sergeant and CEO Davis and Nixon would be on the north end. The deer was placed about a hundred yards from the road.

With everyone in place we began our wait. You never knew whether you would see any vehicles and if you did, not everyone riding through was hunting. However, it was a jam-up spot and my hopes were high that these "new" officers would see some action.

About an hour in, I had a black Chevrolet pickup occupied by two men pass my location and turn toward the detail setup. I radioed Jerry and advised he had one coming. Within about a minute, a shot rang out and Jerry came across the radio saying they had shot. I took off toward the action.

It took me maybe two minutes to reach the scene where the sergeant had the vehicle stopped. It was a little chaotic. The suspects were still in the truck with their hands up. We proceeded to remove them from the truck and handcuff them. Knowing I would be handling part of this investigation, I pulled the lieutenant to the side and ask him to give me the details. He said the driver had shot.

We had hoped to have some success as it would be a great opportunity to train these new officers on what was necessary to make these cases. While I'm sure it sounds relatively open and shut, I learned a long time ago very few cases are that simple. It would turn out to be a good teaching situation.

The officers had removed two high-powered rifles from the truck and secured them in one of our vehicles. I moved the driver to the front of the vehicle and had them take the passenger to the rear. You should always separate the parties as soon as possible. This often prevents them from getting their stories together. When one doesn't know what the other is telling, it makes it difficult for them to match their stories. I know you're thinking their stories would be the same since they were together and both knew what happened. You may be forgetting that folks who have just violated the law often aren't inclined to tell the truth!

Keep in mind this is a fluid situation with a lot going on. As I moved the driver to the front of the truck, I wanted to build some rapport with him if at all possible. I will tell you this is often easier if it's just the two of you and you don't have six officers on the scene. I had to try. Knowing I would want to use anything he said against him, I told the man I needed to talk with him and for his protection I wanted to advise him of his rights. I read him the Miranda warning from a card and he stated he understood. My first question was who this was with him and he reluctantly stated it was his son. As I was moving to my next question, everything was interrupted when the lieutenant located a drug pipe in plain view on the console of the truck. The suspect I was with immediately said, "Tell me she didn't leave that in there!" I have always told new officers one of the best things they can train themselves to do is to listen intently. This was another instance of that. The lieutenant said, "It's a crack pipe." The defendant immediately corrected him and said, "It's a meth pipe." That statement told me he knew exactly what it was and it was going to be hard for him to deny any knowledge of it. I made a mental note.

This actually turned out to be beneficial to me in that it took the defendant's mind off of his rights and sort of loosened him up. He said to me, "I haven't ever done anything like this." Of course, I didn't believe that, but I said, "Tell me about it." He freely told me he and his son were easing down the road and he spotted the deer and it was a "dang good un." I jumped on that and repeated, "A dang good un?" He went on to say he hadn't killed a deer and this was the next-to-last day of the season and it was a dang good un and he shot it. He added that when it didn't go down, he realized it might be a dummy and he took off. Although I would work to get more details, I really had all I needed. I quickly wrote out a statement and had him sign it.

I knew I needed to move to the passenger and the other officers and see what we could get from him. I went to the other officers and asked them what they were thinking as far as charges went and they began listing the possibilities of hunting from the road and from the vehicle and without a permit, which were the proper choices. However, I quickly threw a wrench into their plans when I asked, "And you plan to arrest the passenger too?" A dumbfounded look is probably a good way to describe it. I followed that with the question, "What did you see him do?" This left a lot of blank faces staring at me. I told them, "Let's find out."

I moved to the man's son and asked how old he was and he stated he was twenty-two. I told him I needed to ask him some questions and for his protection I wanted to advise him of his rights and did so. In order to build a little rapport and hopefully get him talking I immediately said, "Your daddy said that was a dang good un." He immediately started laughing. That was a good sign. He said, "That's exactly what he said and I handed him the rifle and he shot it." Believe me when I tell you it normally isn't that easy! In one short statement the fellow revealed that he was a willing participant and contributed significantly to the event by handing his father the gun that he used to shoot the decoy. We went ahead and got a full statement.

I told you I did not believe this was their first time and as it turned out the father had been charged multiple times in the past and the son had actually been apprehended three months earlier doing basically the same thing! So much for never having done anything like that before.

This turned out to be an excellent teaching case. I hope our young officers were paying attention! It really was a dang good un!

Epilogue

WELL, THERE YOU HAVE IT. The culmination of thirty-seven years of working with Game and Fish. It has been a wild ride. While there were definitely some potholes in the road, for the most part it was a good adventure.

I want to thank all of you who have bought these books. I love telling the stories and I hope you've enjoyed this look into my life. As I try to end each book, if you haven't accepted Jesus as your Savior, please consider it today. Having lived in nature, I can tell you this world didn't just happen. It was created by a superior being. Miraculously, He wants us to live with Him through eternity. Accept His offer of eternal life.

In all likelihood, as you read this, I am already in heaven. Despite no history of cancer in my family, I was diagnosed with melanoma. While I was told we caught it early and I underwent immunotherapy, it quickly spread to my brain. Go see your dermatologist! There are no guarantees in this life. Well that's not true. There is one certainty and that is that one out of every one people dies. The question is where will you spend eternity? I was totally blessed with a wonderful wife, family, and friends. Praise the Lord oh my soul. Again I say rejoice.

Thank you all.
Joel D. Glover

Milton Keynes UK
Ingram Content Group UK Ltd.
UKHW021931281024
450365UK00017B/1034

9 780960 046980